PRINCETON ARCHITECTURE

A Pictorial History of
Town and Campus

PRINCETON ARCHITECTURE

A Pictorial History of Town and Campus

CONSTANCE M. GREIFF

MARY W. GIBBONS

ELIZABETH G. C. MENZIES

PRINCETON UNIVERSITY PRESS
PRINCETON, NEW JERSEY

L.C. Card: 65-17138

ISBN 0-691-00583-4 (paperback edn.)

ISBN 0-691-04556-9 (hardcover edn.)

First PRINCETON PAPERBACK Printing, 1975

Printed in the United States of America

PREFACE

IN THE past twenty years Americans have witnessed an unprecedented burst of building activity, frequently combined with heedless destruction of existing structures and landscape. In many ways this change has been creative and fruitful, filling functional and aesthetic needs pent up by depression and war. Too often, however, the result has been a chaos of gaudy strip-cities, Disneyland shopping centers, and characterless suburbs. If there is to be order, if we are to create an environment hospitable to the human spirit and relevant to American experience, we need to take stock of where we have been in order to plan where we are going.

This book grew out of an exhibition calculated to do such a stocktaking of the architectural heritage of one town. The show was mounted in Princeton's Borough Hall in November 1963 in honor of the sesquicentennial of the town's charter. Its purpose was to reveal facets of the town's visual character that few notice in their busy daily life and to show the rich variety that still exists in Princeton. At its conclusion, many viewers of the exhibit expressed the hope that it might be recorded in more permanent form.

For the 1963 show we assembled over four hundred photographs, paintings, drawings, and prints. They were arranged roughly in chronological order, but also grouped to point out significant trends and socio-economic factors. We were aware, of course, of Princeton's important position in the colonial era. What was less obvious, but emerged from the visual material itself, was that Princeton is primarily a nineteenth-century town, imbued with the romanticism of the mid-Victorian years.

Almost every era has produced a scattering of notable buildings in Princeton, perhaps more than could be expected in a town of its size. Under the aegis of a few enlightened institutional and private patrons such distinguished architects as Robert Smith, Benjamin Latrobe, John Haviland, John Notman, Richard Morris Hunt, Ralph Adams Cram, and Minoru Yamasaki have been called upon for commissions. Their work has enriched and enlivened the townscape; but basically Princeton's architecture is provincial and *retardataire*. However the same conservatism that has hampered innovation has served, perhaps without conscious intent, to retain a remarkable panorama of popular taste in building. Unlike Williamsburg, Nantucket, or Philadelphia's Society Hill, Princeton does not preserve the flavor of a particular period. Its chief interest lies in the accuracy with which it reflects the changing tenor of American architecture and life from the late seventeenth century to the present. More than a mere record of fads and fancies, a town's buildings are a testimony to its vitality and development, to its economic ebb and flow, to its commerce as well as to its pleasure. One can read the unfolding of history not only in the pages of a book but in the palpable form of wood and brick.

v

Preface

To select, from the great amount of material assembled for the 1963 show, a representative sampling of illustrations for a book of manageable size was not an easy task. We hoped that the book would be handsome as well as informative and therefore decided to use modern photographs predominantly. Where buildings have disappeared or their original appearance has been distorted by later alterations we have utilized the rich store of Princetoniana available in the Princeton University Library and private collections.

In preparing the exhibition, limitations of time necessitated our dependence on readily available secondary sources for historical background. Although much of the material on Princeton is excellent, we found many contradictions, inaccuracies, and misinterpretations based on insufficient evidence, particularly in the history of the town's early development. Wherever possible, therefore, we have consulted the original sources: newspaper advertisements of properties for sale or rent; letters and diaries; contemporary maps; and official documents of all kinds, letters patent, deeds, and wills. Although specific references to these documents have been excluded from the text, we hope that the note on sources will serve as guide to those readers who wish to pursue further studies in Princeton history.

In our search for information and our efforts to prepare this material for publication we are indebted to many people who gave generously of both time and knowledge. In particular we wish to thank Rosalie B. Green for her help at every stage and her valuable suggestions in connection with reading the manuscript, M. Halsey Thomas, archivist of Princeton University, for his encouragement and the free access he provided to all materials under his aegis, the staff of the Rare Books Department of the Princeton University Library, especially Howard C. Rice, Alfred L. Bush, and Johanna Fantova.

Several members, present and former, of the Department of Art and Archaeology were most helpful in clarifying our ideas about American architecture, in particular, Donald D. Egbert and Virginia W. Egbert, David R. Coffin, William I. Homer, Samuel A. Roberson, Robert H. Rosenblum, and Felton L. Gibbons.

Others whose assistance was most appreciated were Bernard Bush, Alan Gowans, Roger H. McDonough, Rebecca T. Muehleck, Kenneth W. Richards, Henry L. Savage, John Shy, Donald A. Sinclair.

The Vestry of Trinity Church, the Elders of the First Presbyterian Church, and the staff of the Princeton Theological Library, particularly the late Kenneth S. Gapp, kindly allowed us to examine their records.

This book could not have been completed had it not been for the willingness of so many people, too numerous to mention, to allow us to photograph as well as to examine their houses; our warm thanks to all of them.

And finally our special gratitude to Felton, Elizabeth, and David Gibbons, and to Robert, James, and Peter Greiff, who bore our labors with patience and fortitude.

All modern photographs in the book are the work of one of the co-authors, Elizabeth G. C. Menzies. All other illustrative material is from the collections of Princeton University with the following exceptions:

Fig. 4, made available by Bert Gulick; fig. 30, collection of Richard H. Oliphant; fig. 40, the late Hall Park McCullough; fig. 69, Albridge C. Smith, III; fig. 79, from Vol. I of *Lewis Miller, Sketches and Chronicles*, copyright, 1966, by the Historical Society of York County, Pennsylvania.

CONTENTS

A MAP OF MODERN PRINCETON

Showing the Locations of Buildings
Discussed in the Text
By Illustration Numbers

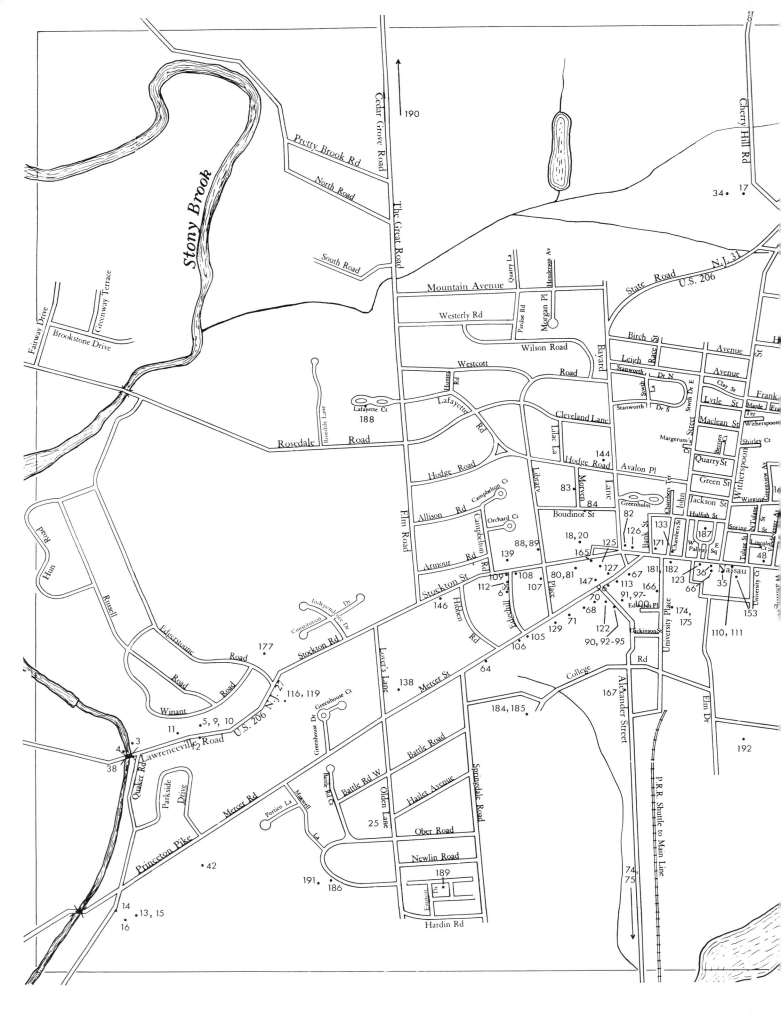

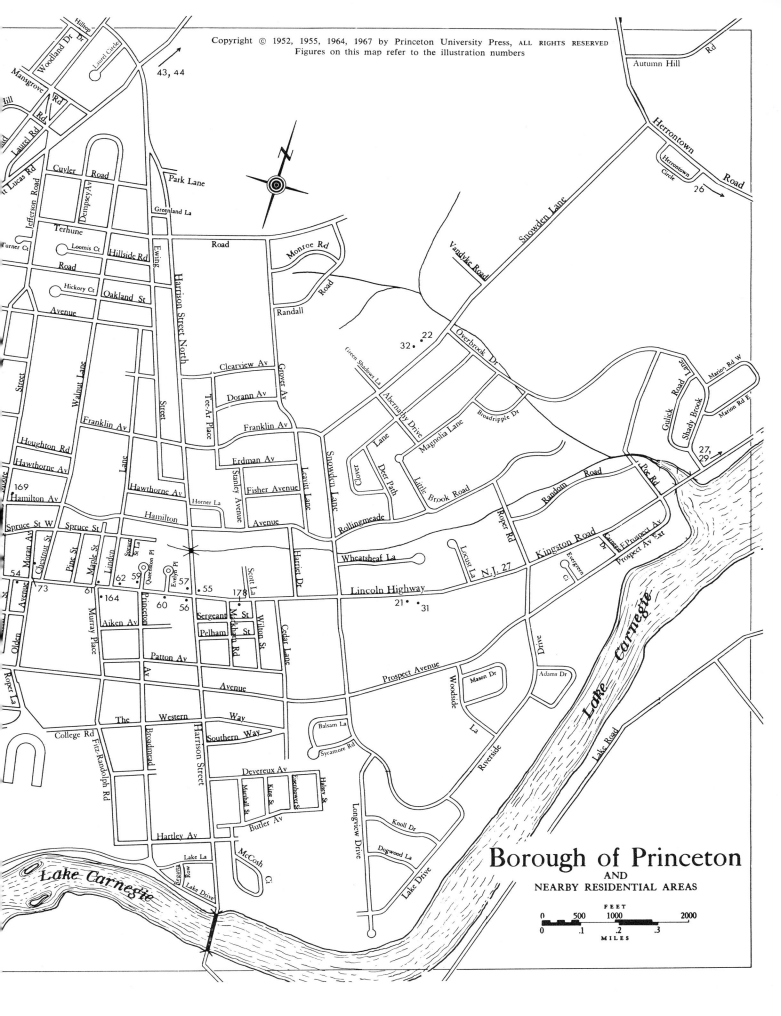

Borough of Princeton
AND
NEARBY RESIDENTIAL AREAS

FEET
0   500   1000   2000

0   .1   .2   .3
MILES

PRINCETON ARCHITECTURE
A Pictorial History of
Town and Campus

I · THE EARLY SETTLEMENT

IN 1675 William Edmundson, a Quaker missionary from England, described the area we now know as Princeton as a "wilderness" in which during a whole day of travel he saw "no tame creature." He must have used the trail the Lenni-Lenape Indians had hacked from the Raritan to the Delaware River. Occasionally the Dutch used this Indian path to carry communications from fur-trading posts on the Hudson River to those on the Delaware. Such infrequent travelers as Sluyter and Danckers, in 1679, described the help given them by friendly Indians along the way in their efforts to ford the Millstone River.

As the settlements on the Hudson gradually spread toward the south and west and those on the Delaware to the north and east, the land of the future Princeton remained a "last frontier" of the Jerseys. New Jersey was owned by co-proprietors, John, Lord Berkeley, and Sir George Carteret. Both men were interested in the colony as a real estate venture and therefore offered very liberal political and religious terms to prospective buyers of their property. Perhaps this encouraged the Scottish Quakers to buy West Jersey from Berkeley in 1675 as a haven for their sect. East Jersey, bought in 1681 from Carteret's estate by William Penn and eleven associates, must have offered similar enticements. When twelve other men bought into the project, East Jersey had twenty-four proprietors of whom twenty were Quakers. The scheme formed part of Penn's grand plan to secure the whole area between the Hudson and Delaware Rivers for the Quakers. Penn tired of this idea, however, preferring to devote his interests exclusively to Pennsylvania and Philadelphia.

The land between the great rivers remained wilderness until the last two decades of the seventeenth century. The earliest settlements in New Jersey quite naturally had followed the courses of the Hudson, Delaware, and Raritan Rivers, all of which have direct access to the sea. Geography was thus one determinant in the lateness of establishing a settlement. Furthermore, during the first three-quarters of the seventeenth century the dividing line between East and West Jersey had not been clearly defined, so that property ownership and titles to land were uncertain. Surely this situation was not encouraging to a prospective settler. The Quintipartite Deed of 1676, which proposed dividing the province on a diagonal line running from Little Egg Harbor on the coast to the northwest corner of the colony, was an attempt to resolve the long-standing confusion about the division. Of much more importance locally was a survey begun in 1685, which resulted in the Keith line of 1687. This eventually became the western boundary of the counties of Middlesex and Somerset and later of the township of Princeton. Its identity is preserved today in Province Line Road. Within five years of the completion of Keith's survey, several of the proprietors took land in the vicinity of the line.

The earliest authoritative account of the settlement of Princeton was written in

1879 by John Frelinghuysen Hageman, a local lawyer. In this history, written in the florid and entertaining style of the Victorian era, Hageman developed the theory that the first settlers of Princeton were all Quakers who, through a preconceived plan, had migrated here as a group. Subsequent writers dealing with various aspects of Princeton's history have perpetuated this idea, along with others derived from Hageman, some of which are well founded, others not. In fact, study of the available seventeenth- and eighteenth-century documents gives us a more complex and varied picture of the early settlement than Hageman's.

When John Reid, assisting Keith in his survey, mapped the area in 1685, Henry Greenland from Piscataway was the only property owner. His two hundred acres lay to the north and west of the Millstone River near Kingston. His residence there is confirmed by the Worlidge Map of 1687-1691, which shows his house on the north side of the road. Greenland's only neighbor was his son-in-law, Daniel Brinson, who then owned land between Springdale and Washington Roads north of Stony Brook. Not long after Henry Greenland had come to the extreme eastern end of the township, a group of Quakers from Chesterfield Meeting bought land along Stony Brook (Fig. 3) at the western edge near the Province Line. Richard Ridgeway, originally from Bucks County, John Houghton, and John Bainbridge each owned several hundred acres of land that lay west of Stony Brook and straddled the Province Line into Lawrence Township. They were all related to the next group of settlers either through Quaker affairs or, in the case of Ridgeway, by marriage. In 1695 John Hornor of Perth Amboy, a relative of several members of the Chesterfield Meeting, acquired five hundred acres between Washington and Harrison Streets. A year later Richard Stockton, who had come from Long Island by way of Burlington and had married Susanna Robinson, a member of the Meeting, purchased land from Daniel Brinson. Brinson seems to have moved to his father-in-law's plantation, which subsequently was left to him and his son, Barefoot, later sheriff of Somerset County. In the same year Benjamin Clarke, who had already migrated from London to Perth Amboy to Piscataway, bought twelve hundred acres at the western end of the township. Almost immediately his two brothers-in-law, William Olden and Joseph Worth, bought pieces of this tract and within a few years moved to Stony Brook.* The last of the seventeenth-century settlers about whom anything is known was Benjamin FitzRandolph from Barnstable, Massachusetts. He had moved to Piscataway, where he became a neighbor of Clarke and his relatives, and then migrated to Princeton, purchasing the three hundred and sixteen acres between Alexander Street and Washington Road from Hornor and Stockton in 1697.

---

* It has usually been assumed that William Olden lived at Stony Brook, but recently examined documents indicate that he resided on a plantation near the Raritan. He wrote his will there in 1719, leaving the Stony Brook plantation to his "ouldest son" John. John settled on the land, willing it to his descendants in 1757. See Fig. 25.

4

The Early Settlement

Although many of these families were related through marriage, religion, or geography, they were not all Quakers, nor did they all come to Stony Brook from the same place at the same time. Rather the pattern of migration followed two main lines, one from the southwest and the other from the northeast. The early settlement between Stony Brook and the Millstone River could be viewed as a microcosm of the pattern of settlement in New Jersey as a whole. Most of the early settlers came from other colonies, working their way gradually inland from the rivers. They brought with them a variety of religions and customs, which made New Jersey, in contrast to Massachusetts or Virginia, a heterogeneous society. These men had a variety of reasons for migrating to the newly-opened Penn tract. Fertile land was available in large or small plots at attractive prices. The streams provided irrigation and water power to run mills. In the surrounding woods there was plenty of timber and stone with which to build houses. The specific topography of the land with the stream along the lower side of the hollow and the trail along the ridge on the upper side made a very convenient arrangement for the settlers. It determined too that the lots would be rather long and narrow, running from the trail at the upper end down to the stream which irrigated the meadows at the lower end. Furthermore, the geographical location seemed to predestine the area's importance as the central point on the main land route from

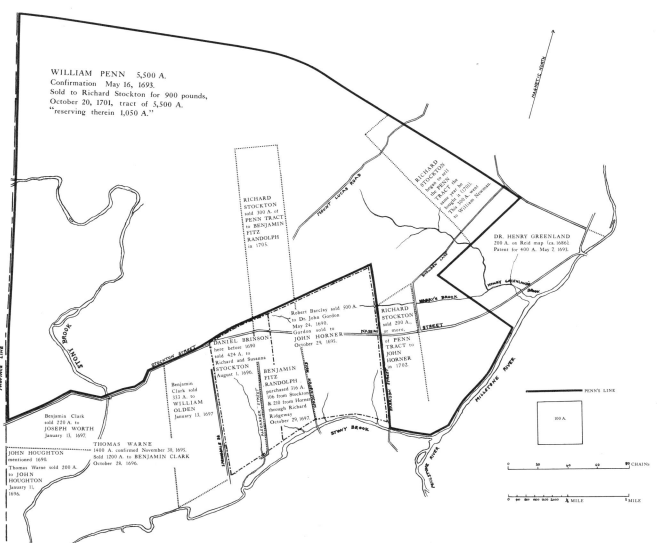

New York to Philadelphia. Not the least of the attractions of this land was the opportunity for those who were Quakers to form an exclusively Quaker community, free from outside interference. Quakers strongly opposed intermarriage with non-Quakers and even disliked close association with others not of their religious persuasion. Perhaps those who came to Stony Brook from Piscataway left the latter place because they were greatly outnumbered by Baptists, whose church was supported by town taxes. Farther south they could form closer ties to their brethren at Chesterfield and the Monthly and Yearly Meetings at Burlington and Philadelphia. They therefore found the hollow in the bend of Stony Brook a perfect home for their close-knit community.

In 1709 Benjamin Clarke gave 9.6 acres for a meeting house and burial ground for the Society of Friends. No immediate action was taken on erecting a building however, and in 1710 the Quarterly Meeting at Burlington approved of settling a meeting at the home of Joseph Worth. In 1724 the Chesterfield Monthly Meeting noted ". . . that it is convenient that a Meeting House for the use of Friends be erected near Stony Brook . . ." and therefore appointed a building committee consisting of Joseph Worth, Benjamin Clarke, Abraham Farrington, John Tantum, and Thomas Lambert. They recommended that the building be of stone, that it measure thirty by thirty-four feet, and that it be erected for a sum not to exceed one hundred and fifty pounds. This edifice was severely damaged by fire in 1758-1759 but rebuilt on the same foundations in 1760. The present building (Fig. 15), still in use, undoubtedly bears a close resemblance to the original. In 1781 the Friends built a house for a schoolmaster on the Meeting House property.

The scattering of houses located between the Millstone River and Stony Brook was not called Princeton until 1724. Before that time the settlers described themselves as "of Stony Brook," "of Piscataway," or "of Millstone." Indeed until 1724 the only sense of community derived from the small group of Quakers. Bound together by their common faith, the Stony Brook Quakers organized their community life around the Meeting House. The Meeting functioned not only as the spiritual center of the settlement but also as its welfare department, civil court, and social arbiter. Thus the Meeting House became the most important building in the village.

Between 1712 and 1715 the first industry came to Stony Brook. In 1712 Thomas Potts, a miller from Pennsylvania, secured the deed for a mill pond with the right to dig a raceway. Two years later Potts bought enough land from Joseph Worth to build two grist mills and a bolting mill. This meant that grain could be ground locally into flour and feed. Previously the closest mill had been Harrison's at Rocky Hill. These mills soon reverted to the Worth family; they remained in operation until early in the twentieth century (Fig. 4). Today only a crumbling wall remains to mark the site of this first business enterprise at Stony Brook. On the road below the mill a bridge was built in 1738, for by this time the horse track through the forest had been widened and crude carts and pack horses could carry the produce of the mill to tidewater. Even a stagecoach could now make the journey from Trenton to New Brunswick.

No buildings have survived from the first Princeton settlements. However we can tell from written records and the few seventeenth-century houses that remain in other parts of the United States what sort of dwellings the settlers built. When William Olden, Richard Stockton, and Henry Greenland arrived they needed shelter quickly. Contrary to legend, they did not build log cabins.* We are given a vivid description of the early shelters by one of the East Jersey proprietors, Gawen Lawrie, who wrote in 1684, "The country farm houses are built very cheap. A carpenter, with a man's own servants builds the house; they have all materials for nothing, except nails, their chimnies are of stones. . . . The poor sort set up a house of two or three rooms themselves, after this manner; the walls are of cloven timber, about eight or ten inches broad, like planks, set one end to the ground and the other nailed to the raising which they plaister within." Others used arbors or dug-outs for their first temporary dwellings.

After the initial tasks of settling were completed—the land cleared, the farming begun—the settlers began to build more permanent houses. Even this second stage of building, though more substantial, was still very primitive and simple. Parts of the houses of this second stage were incorporated in later structures. In the center section of the Gulick Farm on Kingston Road (Fig. 27) lies buried what was probably part of the house of Henry Greenland, the first settler. The original Olden House is quite likely a part of what is now known as Olden Manor (Fig. 25). Glimpses of structural detail, a hand-hewn beam, a rough stone wall, or an enormous fireplace, give clues to identification of these old portions. One of the earliest extant houses, The Barracks (Fig. 6), traditionally called the oldest house in Princeton, still preserves, buried within later additions, part of the original Richard Stockton house, which stood very near the overland trail. This is the "dwelling plantation" left by Richard to his son John in 1709, and in which John lived until he died. Built of native fieldstone, it was well adapted to serve as one of the first farms in the Stony Brook settlement. The little Thomas Olden house on Stockton Street (Fig. 8), although not so early in date, is the kind of house that Joseph Worth might have built for his family in about 1700; the small one-story frame building with windows and doors placed only where necessary fulfilled the needs of the early colonist.

These structures, both public and private, erected at or near the Stony Brook settlement in the late seventeenth and early eighteenth centuries represent a style of building, not really architecture, which the colonists brought from England and the Continent. It was the same kind of vernacular building that served the bourgeoisie

* Log houses or cabins appeared in America only in two forms, either as block houses in fortified settlements or as an indigenous form used by the Scandinavians who settled along the lower Delaware. The influence of the Scandinavian log cabin type spread gradually until late in the eighteenth century, when it became the common frontier architecture of America.

and farmers in counties of England such as East Anglia. Often called "medieval" in style because of its unconscious disregard for symmetry, its lack of formality, and its preference for a rambling irregular silhouette, it would perhaps be more accurate to call it preclassical building. Unlike Massachusetts or Virginia, the central part of New Jersey has no pronounced regional characteristics in building nor any single style identified with it. It is virtually impossible to find an example of a house in this area that can with certainty be considered of pure Dutch or English derivation, for example. Just as the country as a whole has been called a melting pot of European peoples, so this part of central New Jersey might be called a melting pot of colonial architecture. The first settlers who came here did not migrate directly from their mother countries, but came rather from other colonies in the New World or from other parts of New Jersey. The Stockton family, for example, had settled first on Long Island and then at Burlington before finally coming to Stony Brook. Thus these colonists brought with them not only the building traditions of their homelands but also those of other colonies where there were English, Dutch, Flemish, and Swedish settlers. The local style then combined the characteristics which they had found most useful and appealing in their previous experiences. They used the masonry preferred in New Netherland and in the Quaker settlements along the Delaware as well as the clapboard over half timber construction favored by the English. The most popular floor plan seems to derive from New Netherland houses in which the rooms extended laterally from the original one-room house. The chimneys were either built into the side walls of the house or occasionally put in the corners of the rooms, a motif found primarily in the Delaware Valley. Such a heterogeneous style was perhaps expressive of the experience of these settlers and showed them to be adaptable to various environments.

What holds true for all of central New Jersey is equally true of Princeton. The local style of building was a mixture, but marked by some distinctive, though minor, characteristics. In wooden buildings the lower masonry of the chimney was often left exposed, set into the clapboard sidewall. This usage was exceptionally popular in the Princeton area and persisted throughout the eighteenth century. The strung-out "Dutch" floor plan, two to four times as long as wide, was combined with the un-"Dutch" characteristic of a high second story, crowned with a gable roof. This combination of long plan with relatively high elevation resulted in houses of distinctly vertical proportions; these were so popular in the area that they persisted for years and were later accentuated in the early Victorian style of the nineteenth century.

Throughout the American colonies, whether in Massachusetts, New York, or New Jersey, the early settlers built to suit their daily needs without any conscious regard for the appearance of their buildings. They achieved a functionalism in their architecture which is very appealing to the modern eye, so disdainful of superfluous ornament or arbitrary symmetry. Frontier life demanded simple and economical solutions to building needs. Life was not yet complicated by wealth and its concomitant desires to show status and sophistication. The humble seventeenth-century house might consist of only one room, the hall or keeping-room with loft above, where life centered around a large open fireplace. Here the family ate, sat, worked, and even slept. If slightly grander, the house might have a parlor in which to entertain the minister or other important guests, and one or two bedrooms. The Thomas Olden house (Fig. 8) resembles one of these simple early houses. The asymmetrical placement of the windows and doors, the lack of any emphasis on or centralization of the main door, the smallness of the house itself, all bespeak its sole function as a dwelling. The interior arrangements of the house are all directly revealed on the exterior. The closeness of its relationship to its surroundings is expressed by the way in which it hugs the ground. The Quaker Meeting House too (Figs. 13, 15), despite the Early Georgian characteristics of symmetry and marking of horizontal and vertical axes, exhibits this direct attitude toward building. In its use of undressed native fieldstone, its simple rectangular shape, it belongs to the period of building in which structure and plan were revealed through the undisguised handling of the materials provided by nature. No attempt was made in these early buildings to hide the inherent qualities of the materials used. Often the interior cellar beams of houses were whole tree trunks on which the bark still remained. Surely the Quaker and Puritan preference for plain unadorned dress had its counterpart in their buildings. Whatever beauty their architecture possessed derived from its qualities of craftsmanship, frank expression of materials, solid construction, and austere design.

1. Confluence of Harry's Brook and Lake Carnegie. Sometime
before 1685 Henry Greenland settled on a plot at the eastern
end of what is now Princeton Township. His land was bordered
on the southeast by the Millstone River (which was widened
in 1906 to make Lake Carnegie). On the west it was watered
by the stream still known as Harry's Brook, designated on the
Dalley Map of 1745 (New York Historical Society copy) as
"H: Greenland's Brook." By 1766, when Azariah Dunham
mapped the division line between Somerset and Middlesex
Counties, the form "Harry's Brook" was already in use.

2. North shore of Lake Carnegie, looking east toward the Washington Road Bridge. This land was first settled by John Hornor. Benjamin FitzRandolph purchased it, along with an adjoining parcel from Richard Stockton, in 1697. FitzRandolph's east and west boundaries still affect Princeton's map, transmuted into Springdale and Washington Roads. Like most of the early plots, FitzRandolph's ran roughly north from Stony Brook to border or include the only thoroughfare, the modern Nassau Street. The fertile meadow lots along the river were particularly desirable; they were often divided among heirs as parcels separate from other holdings.

3. Stony Brook, looking downstream toward the Stockton Street crossing. Legend to the contrary, Stony Brook was not named in nostalgic reminiscence of another stream. The Stockton family's previous residence had been at Flushing, many miles distant from Stony Brook, Long Island. Princeton's Stony Brook appears as such on the map drawn by John Reid in 1685. The name was probably simply descriptive. The western bend of Stony Brook became the center of Princeton's Quaker settlement. As early as 1690 John Houghton from Chesterfield Meeting owned land along its west bank. Six years later Benjamin Clarke purchased 1200 acres on the east side of the river from Thomas Warne, one of the Proprietors of East Jersey. Almost immediately Clarke conveyed part of his tract to his brothers-in-law, William Olden and Joseph Worth. Clarke and Worth were instrumental in establishing a Preparative Meeting of Friends at Stony Brook.

4. Worth's Mill and the Stockton Street Bridge. Although
Joseph Worth purchased his land in 1696, he apparently did
not move to Stony Brook immediately. His second child, Giles,
was born in Piscataway at the end of 1697; his third, Sarah,
at Stony Brook early in 1700. In 1716 he purchased the grist
mill built by a Pennsylvania miller, Thomas Potts, two years
earlier. It remained in the hands of Worth's descendants and
in continuous operation until the early years of the twentieth
century. All that now remains of the mill is a crumbling stone
wall. The bridge was erected in 1792, replacing one destroyed
during the Battle of Princeton.

5. 487 and 481 Stockton Street. The inhabitants of the western
end of what is now Princeton Township continued to refer to
themselves as "of Stony Brook" long after 1724 when the name
Princeton was first applied to the other little cluster of buildings two miles east along the road. In 1781 the French cartographer Louis-Alexandre Berthier, mapping the route of Rochambeau's Army from the Hudson River to Yorktown, called this
area "Stony brug hameau." Although its separate identity has
been lost in succeeding years, traces of its character remain in
the small scale and unpretentious proportion and detailing of
its early buildings.

6

7

8. Thomas Olden House, 344 Stockton Street. This house has been moved three hundred yards to the north from its original site. Like most early farmhouses it is difficult to date. Similar simple forms and informal additive compositions were used throughout the eighteenth century by all but the most affluent. In outbuildings and the humblest dwellings these characteristics persisted well into the nineteenth century. It is likely, however, that the Thomas Olden House was built before the Revolution; Thomas Olden acquired the property from his father, by inheritance, in 1757, and the interior detail is typical of the style of the mid-eighteenth century.

6. The Barracks, 32 Edgehill Street. The wing at the right (partly concealed) and the entry are modern additions. This is certainly one of the oldest houses in Princeton. It appears on all the early maps of the area and is described in eighteenth-century deeds and real estate advertisements. It was probably built by one of the early owners of the property on which it stands, Daniel Brinson, whose deed is dated 10 February 1685/6, or Richard Stockton, who purchased the land in 1696. It is the "dwelling plantation" left by Richard to his son John in 1709, in which John Stockton lived until his death in 1758.

7. Detail of beam in the basement of The Barracks. Few seventeenth- and eighteenth-century buildings have escaped deletions, additions, and alterations. The Barracks is no exception. In the eighteenth century it was twice as large. Traces can be seen of rearrangement of rooms within and changes in placement of doors and windows without. The lintels are of a type not used before the middle of the eighteenth century; the six-over-six sash probably dates from the early nineteenth century. Often attics and basements are least affected by changes in fashion. Unadzed tree trunks used as beams still remain in the basement of The Barracks, a clue to the building's early date.

9. 487 Stockton Street

10. 481 Stockton Street

At least a portion of each of these houses dates from the eighteenth century. Except for 481, all appear on both the Berthier map and in a travel directory published in 1804. According to tradition the foundations of 481 are those of a smithy, 487 having been the blacksmith's residence. This is confirmed by the 1804 map as well as by a contemporary account of the misadventures suffered by a blacksmith from this vicinity during the Revolution. All but 487 seem to have been added to and much altered in the early part of the nineteenth century. In material, silhouette, and proportion, 487 is strongly reminiscent of houses to be found in the Quaker settlements on the west side of the Delaware.

12. 498 Stockton Street

11. 537 Stockton Street

13. Quaker Meeting House, interior. The simple but handsome lines and details have remained largely unaltered since the construction of the Meeting House. Vertical beaded wainscoting; facing benches and pews; twelve-over-twelve sash windows with much of the original glass; gallery; and winding in-wall staircase all remain intact. The long silences of Meeting must have been a strain for some members, for benches, posts supporting the gallery, and gallery rails are covered with initials, dates and drawings. One of the longest inscriptions, in the loft, reads, "R. H. Princeton August ADomini 1790 Quarterly Meeting."

14. Schoolmaster's House, Quaker Meeting. This house, part of which was erected as a residence for a schoolmaster in 1781, is the only visible remainder of the Stony Brook School. The one room schoolhouse, which stood near the Meeting House, was torn down in 1901. The Friends' concern for education was deep. Benjamin Clarke's will specified that ". . . my children shall have good learning and be brought up in a Christian like manner. . . ."

15. The Quaker Meeting House. When the original building, erected in 1724, was severely damaged, probably by fire, in December 1759, the present Meeting House was built as a replacement. It duplicated the dimensions of the earlier structure, approximately 30 by 34 feet. In all likelihood it resembles it closely in other aspects as well. Although the centralization of the single door and the balanced placing of windows on either side of the façade are symptomatic of the more formal planning of Georgian architecture, the building's extreme simplicity, verticality, and direct handling of materials retain the stamp of early domestic building types. Details that can be associated with the Georgian style, such as the water table and the segmental arched window headings, seem more closely related to the Georgian of the second decade of the eighteenth century than of the third. One of the most attractive features of the Meeting is the warm yellowish sandstone, similar to that used at Nassau Hall. In all probability the same mason, William Worth, was responsible for the stonework of both. The wooden porch is a later addition. During the Revolutionary War the Meeting House was used as a temporary field hospital after the Battle of Princeton. Its benches and floor still bear dark stains, reputed to be the blood of the wounded. The Meeting House remained in use through the first half of the nineteenth century. Gradually, however, its membership declined and in the 1870's it was closed, except for rare occasions. After a hiatus of about seventy years it was reopened and is now in regular use for First Day Meeting.

16. In the quiet graveyard lie members of Princeton's pioneering families. According to Quaker custom most of the early graves are unmarked; later rough fieldstones bear crudely incised initials or names. The stone wall surrounding the graveyard was built in 1859.

17. Tusculum, Cherry Hill Road. John Witherspoon built his "neat and elegantly finished" country house in 1773. For a few years he rented it, noting however that ". . . the Proprietor being fond of agriculture and engag'd in a scheme of improvement, will not let any of the land for tillage. . . ." Tusculum is simple country Georgian, revealing its late date only in its generous expanses of glass. The house has passed through many hands and many remodelings, including a Victorian mask of bay windows and gingerbread. It has been carefully restored by its present owner to an approximation of its original appearance.

II · MANOR HOUSES AND YEOMAN FARMS

THE gradual growth of population in the Stony Brook community and the surrounding countryside during the early eighteenth century changed Princeton from wilderness to cultivated farmland. At the same time, such rivers as the Millstone and Stony Brook were bridged, and traffic overland across the waist of New Jersey increased. One of the early travelers, Professor Peter Kalm, wrote, in 1748, "About ten o'clock in the morning we came to Princeton, which is situated in a plain. Most of the houses are built of wood, and are not contiguous, so that there are gardens and pastures between them. As these parts were sooner inhabited by Europeans than Pennsylvania, the woods were likewise more cut away, and the country more cultivated, so that one might have imagined himself to be in Europe." Although Kalm was wrong about the priority of settlement, his comments are relevant. Central New Jersey remained primarily agricultural throughout the eighteenth century. In the plain cradled by Stony Brook and the Millstone River the average farm comprised about two hundred acres. This was larger than farms in East Jersey, but smaller than those in West Jersey. The size of farms was crucial in colonial New Jersey, since one's vote depended on one's acreage. Before 1709 the franchise was granted only to owners of one hundred acres or more and a seat in the Assembly only to holders of one thousand acres or more. After 1709, however, the laws were liberalized to grant suffrage to anyone who owned real or personal property worth at least fifty dollars; but ownership of land still carried with it political power.

Princeton was not founded by men of the aristocracy. On the contrary, the earliest settlers described themselves as yeomen, not gentlemen; and we know, for example, that Joseph Worth was a cooper, Benjamin FitzRandolph a carpenter, and Richard Ridgeway a tailor. A farm belonging to one of these men would have been worked by the family with the help of one or two slaves or indentured servants. The few wealthier members of the community—Greenland, surgeon and innkeeper; Clarke, son of a stationer; and Richard Stockton—needed more labor on their larger farms. Benjamin Clarke, who was wealthy enough to make generous gifts to the Meeting, had several indentured servants, and Richard Stockton needed more than seven slaves to till his land. Hired labor was unavailable because land was so plentiful that each free man could own his own plot.

To make a success of a farm required prudent management by the owner. Bankruptcies and sales for debt were not uncommon. Thomas Leonard, who acquired more than three thousand acres of land through his marriage to Susannah Stockton, the wealthy widow of the first Richard, died a debtor. Samuel Stockton's lands and tenements, containing more than two hundred acres and a "good new Brick House," were sold at a sheriff's sale in 1764. But John Stockton's eldest son, Richard the Signer, so called because he signed the Declaration of Independence, must have been a very careful and successful manager. In a letter to his wife Annis written from England and reporting on his attendance at the Queen's Birthday Ball and on his purchases, he did not forget to give her instructions on shoes for the slaves and proper pasturage for the cattle.

Benjamin Clarke, Richard Stockton, and others who owned large tracts of land often used the term "plantation" in their deeds or other business transactions, but they were not gentlemen farmers nor did they live in a plantation society. "Plantation" to them meant any planted area as distinguished from undeveloped land; it was synonymous with "farm": the two words are used interchangeably in newspaper advertisements of the day.

As mid-century approached, frontier conditions no longer existed in the settlement; life became physically and economically easier. Often a man was both farmer and lawyer like Richard Stockton, or farmer and merchant, or farmer and miller like Joseph Worth. But he could never ignore his farm. The men who settled Princeton were industrious, serious-minded, middleclass people who founded an agricultural community out of which grew a small town of tradesmen, farmers, and soon intellectuals. The settlement never had the aristocratic overtones so characteristic of the southern part of America.

After the settlers emerged from their first successful struggles in taming the wilderness, they naturally began to think of making themselves more comfortable. First of all they needed more space in which to live. To achieve this they gradually added rooms to their original houses. The architectural style was still vernacular, still utterly functional and simple, and it continued to be so throughout the eighteenth century, even after the new Georgian style appeared. Thus it is often difficult to date a building like the Greenland-Brinson-Gulick house at 1082 Princeton-Kingston Road (Fig. 27). The center section of this house, which is one small room with loft above, probably dates from the seventeenth century. The roof of the original section was raised during the eighteenth century to conform to a new wing added at the west end. The eighteenth-century wing is a typical two-story farmhouse of the time, rather long and narrow in proportions. In the late eighteenth or early nineteenth century a Federal style wing was added containing a stair hall and double parlors. Olden Manor on Olden Lane (Fig. 25) and the Clarke house on Quaker Road tell the same story of increasing prosperity.

With growing affluence the colonists of Stony Brook began to think of themselves in grander terms. The first Benjamin Clarke in his will of March 15, 1747, described himself simply as "of Stony Brook . . . Yeoman." His son, Benjamin, in his will of September of the same year, omitted the "yeoman" and referred to his dwelling as his "mansion house at Stony Brook." Thomas Leonard, who must have had the grandest house in the vicinity, is designated on the Dalley map of 1745 as "Esquire": his house, described as "his Seat at Grove Hall," is three times larger than any other

24

building on the map. By mid-century the houses were not all of timber or native fieldstone but sometimes of brick. Nathaniel FitzRandolph precisely described the advent of his fourteenth child, Elizabeth, "near Princeton in my brick house on Tuseday night about midnight february ye 15th 1757: New Stile." When he was, unfortunately, forced to put the house up for sale in 1763, he described it as "four Rooms on the lower Floor, four Fire Places, a Cellar all under . . . fronting the College in fair view."

The development of a farm economy and the gradual change in architectural style that coincided with the increasing prosperity of the settlement at Stony Brook are vividly illustrated by the history of the Stockton family. At his death in 1709 the first Richard Stockton had willed his land, divided into various lots, to his sons. John, the fifth son, inherited his father's "dwelling plantation." Contrary to the long tradition begun by Hageman in 1879, the dwelling plantation deeded to John in the will of 1709 was not Morven. What John inherited from his father was the land on which Morven stands today and that on which The Barracks stands. An interesting chain of evidence plus a consideration of the architectural style of Morven (Fig. 20) places the house securely in its proper chronological place, the mid-eighteenth century. Neither the Emley survey, drawn in 1709 to show the distribution of the elder Richard's property, nor the Dalley map of 1745 shows Morven in existence. The Barracks (Fig. 6), however, which appears on both of these maps, is marked on the latter as the home of John Stockton. Morven appears for the first time on the Dunham map of 1766, which indicates also that The Barracks was at that time owned by Ezekiel Forman. Both houses appear on the "spy" map of 1776-1777, where The Barracks is designated as the "old Stockton place." From the deed by which the land on which Morven was built was conveyed to Richard the Signer in 1754 it is quite clear that his father, John Stockton, lived in The Barracks. On May 1, 1764, Richard the Signer conveyed to Ezekiel Forman the "homestead farm of John Stockton, Esq." The Barracks, then, which preserves a vestige of one of the earliest houses in Princeton, has the added distinction of having been the first home of Princeton's first family for two generations. Only four years after he bought it in 1764, Ezekiel Forman offered it for sale, leaving an excellent description of what the original house must have been. It was a farm of three-hundred-ten acres containing "A stone dwelling house two stories high, ninety feet in length, by twenty-five; five rooms on the lower floor, and as many fire-places; six rooms on the second floor (exclusive of the servants lodging rooms) . . . the whole, plain, but neatly finished . . . kitchen garden . . . well finished Dutch barn forty four by forty feet," stable for cattle, wagon house, cider house, and other outbuildings. Though very characteristic of the vernacular style in its utilitarian, asymmetrical plan, The Barracks with its eleven rooms had by 1768 already begun to show the prosperity of the Stockton family.

In contrast to The Barracks, Morven, romantically named by Annis and Richard the Signer after the mythical home of Fingal in Macpherson's *Ossian,* is representative of the new age that was already half a century old in Europe by mid-eighteenth century. Its style is entirely compatible with the date of 1754-1755, a date that agrees with the documents just cited. Although the house has undergone numerous restorations and modifications since it was built, it retains enough general eighteenth-century elements to be a valid object of study. It is a fully-developed though provincial example of the Georgian style that even then was relatively new in the Colonies. A date as early as the traditional one of 1701 would not only conflict with this evidence but would make Morven a contemporary of the Capitol and earlier than the Governor's Palace at Williamsburg, one of the undisputed leaders of the new style in the New World.

Georgian architecture, derived from the late sixteenth-century Italian architect Palladio, first brought to England by Inigo Jones in the second decade of the seventeenth century, and later modified and highly popularized by Sir Christopher Wren in his rebuilding of London after the Great Fire of 1666, became very popular in America. It was transmitted throughout England and the Colonies primarily by the publication of architectural books by Palladio, James Gibbs, Isaac Ware, Batty Langley, and Abraham Swan. It has, in fact, never died in the United States and even today continues to be imitated in a much adulterated form.

Men like Richard Stockton the Signer, who had begun to feel the importance of their newly-acquired wealth and social position, were no longer content to build their houses in the purely functional primitive style of their fathers and grandfathers. No longer restricted by the exigencies of a frontier society, they desired to express their social status and political importance in some visible way. Richard Stockton and others like him were highly educated men who counted a knowledge of architecture as one of the attainments of a gentleman. They set out to emulate the best that the mother country could produce in elegance and sophistication. Georgian architecture, highly rational and formal, expressed the mind of the Age of Enlightenment, in which man was thought to be no longer subject to the whims of God and nature, and in which he felt capable of bringing a high measure of order to society. He intended to impose his will on nature. Nowhere is this new feeling better expressed than in the architecture of the period.

Morven embodies the new social attitudes and cultural aspirations of a small but increasingly important mid-eighteenth-century class in America. Discarding functionalism in a desire to express a formal and elegant way of life, the well-to-do in Princeton, as in other towns of the New World, seized on the Georgian style as the answer to their needs. The ground plan of a house such as Morven clearly demonstrates the new concern for pure form, symmetry, and greater amplitude in living arrangements. The old all-purpose hall of the primitive houses has been replaced by a wide,

26

impressive entrance hallway leading from the main door of the house to the rear door opposite. This was carefully calculated to give the visitor an uninterrupted view of the garden beyond the house, as well as to allow privacy to the rooms flanking the hall. The rooms on the ground floor, now differentiated in function, were balanced in plan. This typical Georgian ground plan has been in continuous use in the United States for two hundred years. Morven's slight variation, relegating the stairs to a separate sidehall, occurs in a few scattered instances elsewhere in the colonies but, it is interesting to note, with particular frequency in a group of houses in and near Philadelphia.*

The exterior units of Georgian houses, like the interior, were meticulously calculated to provide a sense of balance. Although the three sections of Morven, central block with two wings, were not built simultaneously, the house evolved into a balanced complex consisting of three distinct but coordinated units. Structural details indicate that the west wing was the earliest construction. The central block was added after 1754, and sometime after this, probably in the late eighteenth century, the east wing was added to balance the west. It is even possible that the three stages of building at Morven took place during the lifetime of Richard the Signer.

As an expression of a self-conscious quest for classic perfection in architecture the façade of Morven deserves attention. It reiterates the diagrammatic clarity of the floor plan. The large, evenly-spaced windows produce a measured rhythm which is uninterrupted save for the front entrance, whose location in the center of the façade and accentuation by size and trimming provide the chief organizing factor. Convenience and economy have been cast aside in favor of symmetry and formal pattern. The scale is larger than in the pre-classic age; and although ceiling heights are increased the stress is now on horizontality rather than verticality. The horizontal emphasis is achieved by a lower-pitched roof, carved cornice, stringcourse, and window trimming. The façade is composed of simple geometric shapes, smooth surfaces, and distinct outlines.

In choosing a material for constructing Morven, the builder selected brick, a man-made medium which he could control and produce in regular, clear-cut shapes. Rough-hewn timbers or uncut native stone were not adapted to the new desire for regularity. Brick was ideal, for it could be manipulated to create its own rectilinear pattern, which then reinforced the formal design of the whole house. At Morven, as in other Georgian houses, carefully-cut stone and carved wood were commonly used for trim. Before the addition of the portico the house must have looked striking, with the formal elements of the façade stressed by the contrast of painted woodwork

* Of these Trent House (1719) in Trenton, New Jersey, and Hope Lodge (1745-1760) in White Marsh, Pennsylvania, are earlier than Morven, while Mount Pleasant (1761-1762) in Philadelphia and Port Royal (1762) in Frankfort, Pennsylvania, are later.

against red brick. At a glance one could encompass this façade and understand the relations of its component parts.

In Philadelphia, which was architecturally one of the most progressive cities of the colonies, houses had been built of brick since the founding. But one cannot date any brick house in Princeton before the mid-1750's, when Robert Smith came from Philadelphia to build for the college. Brick was obviously thought of as a luxury material. Even in Boston in the late eighteenth century, Charles Bulfinch found it difficult to persuade his thrifty Yankee patrons to use brick for their houses.

Along with the thoughtfully planned and executed design of the Georgian house went equally important considerations of site and orientation. A Georgian house was meant to be easily seen, respectfully approached, and in harmony with its surroundings. Morven, set on a relatively high foundation with half the basement visible, seems master of all it surveys. The house stands out clearly from its site and frankly dominates it, but a perfectly easy harmony is maintained. In laying out the gardens of Morven, Annis and Richard Stockton sought to enhance the house and beautify its grounds by selecting ornamental trees, shrubs, and flowers. They were guided in their plans by ideas Richard acquired when he visited Alexander Pope's garden in Twickenham with the express purpose of having a drawing made to bring back with him to Princeton. And Annis, in one of her numerous poems, reflects the eighteenth-century concern for propriety in nature, a sense of an overall design in which each part is purposefully placed according to its beauty or function. She writes,

> While fruits and flowers so nicely are displayed,
> As if the powers of order here had made
> Their chosen seat: while usefullness combin'd
> Gives us the portrait of the farmer's mind.
> Thus mighty Rome's fam'd orators of old,
> In counsel deep, and in the senate bold,
> Defending innocence from lawless force,
> And guiding justice to its proper source,
> Could quit the forum for the Sabine field,
> With their own hand the spade and plough could wield,
> And in their gardens every lux'ry plac'd
> That nature gives to elegance and taste.

Morven was the grandest of Princeton's country houses, but there were others that shared some of its characteristics. The mid-eighteenth-century Constitution Hill (Fig. 23) (now destroyed) and Castle Howard (Fig. 21), while preserving the proportions of the primitive farmhouse type and using less formal building materials, nevertheless had the high basements and symmetrical façades typical of the new style. At Maybury Hill (Fig. 22) on Snowden Lane, in order to conform to the new fashion, a Georgian

28

façade was superimposed on the two early wings of the house. Three other houses that fall into the category of great farms but represent a slightly different type are Mansgrove on Mount Lucas Road (Fig. 24), the Scott House on Herrontown Road (Fig. 26), and the Greenland-Brinson-Gulick house (Fig. 27). In these houses, a larger, more important post-Revolutionary section, characterized by delicate, attenuated, Adamesque detail, has been added to an existing earlier structure that usually became the service wing of the grander house.

During the course of the second half of the eighteenth century the Stocktons were joined by other increasingly prosperous families to form a landed gentry in Princeton. While attending with one hand to the management of their lands, with the other they were able to find leisure for intellectual, political, and social pursuits of life unknown to their fathers and grandfathers. Gradually their interests and their outlooks broadened to include service to their town, to their province, and finally to their nation. Richard the Signer is, of course, the most famous of his local contemporaries for his part in signing the Declaration of Independence. But there were others like Thomas Leonard and Nathaniel FitzRandolph who were enlightened enough to devote their energies to luring the infant College of New Jersey to Princeton.

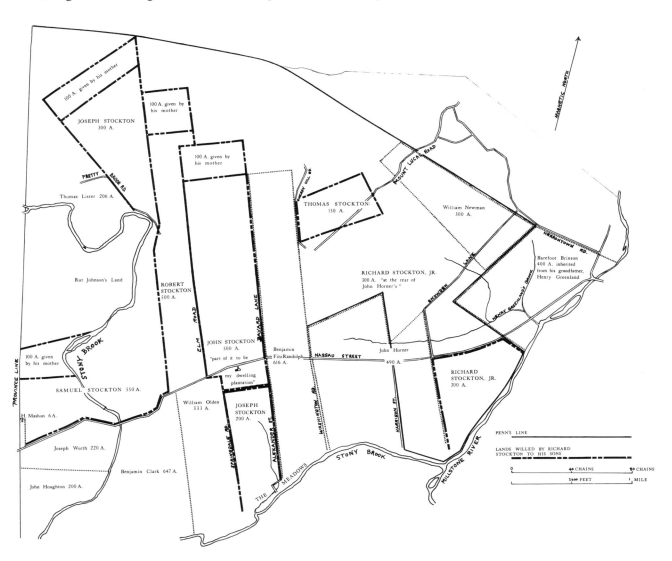

18. Morven, detail, doorway. Like many Georgian houses, Morven has undergone numerous remodelings and renovations since it was built by Richard Stockton the Signer sometime after 1754. The doorway is of a type which became most popular in this country toward the end of the eighteenth century; it probably dates from a general refurbishing that seems to have been undertaken after the Revolution. So too does the veranda, to which Annis Stockton made several references, calling it a "piazza," in letters written in 1790 and 1791. The impetus for this post-Revolutionary building program may have been the necessity of repairing damage done to the house during its occupancy by the British in 1776, although the persistent legend that the British burned the east wing is not corroborated by documentary evidence. That wing was destroyed, however, by a fire in 1821. Its reconstruction was probably entrusted to Charles Steadman; its staircase is similar to those in several of his buildings and Hageman, in enumerating the houses built by Steadman on Stockton Street, specifically excepts the "original part" of Morven. In 1848 Commodore Robert F. Stockton renovated Morven, raising the wings from their original height of one story to two and substantially replacing the original woodwork with Victorian decor. In the past seventy years, successive owners have restored Morven to something resembling its colonial appearance, although little of the original fabric, beyond the plan, walls, and major partitions, remains.

19. In mapping a possible campsite for Rochambeau's troops in 1781, Berthier also sketched the siting and exterior arrangements of the two Stockton homesteads, The Barracks and Morven. The former appears as a utilitarian farm. Approached by a lane (now Edgehill Street), it is surrounded by cultivated fields which extend to the immediate vicinity of the house. Close to the house is another structure almost as big, evidently the "well-finished Dutch barn" described by Ezekiel Forman when he offered the property for sale in 1768. In contrast, Morven is oriented to the road, with the immediately surrounding property laid out to form a clearly delineated rectangle. Within this basic shape, simple symmetrical forms have been employed in laying out a garden. There are no indications of fields or outbuildings, although Morven was a working farm. Elegant and aloof, the house stood isolated from its occupants' mundane activities, alone in its formal setting.

18

19

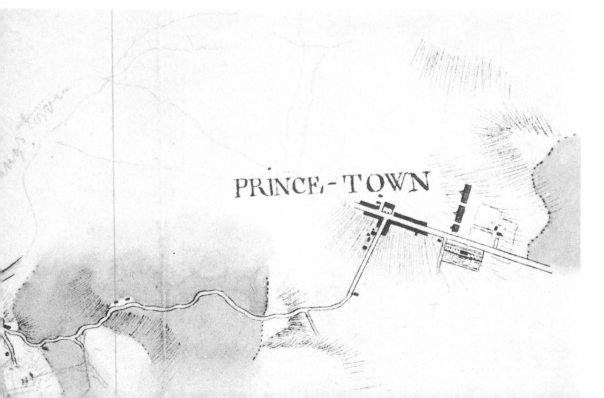

PRINCE-TOWN

20. Morven, overleaf

21. Castle Howard, Princeton-Kingston Road, stands on property left by the earliest Stockton settler, Richard, to his eldest son Richard, uncle of the Signer. While the small wing to the left may be earlier, the larger portion of the house must have been built c. 1760, for it was advertised for sale in 1763 as a ". . . commodious new Stone House, well finished, with a good Stone Kitchen, and a Piazza . . . ," the latter a rare feature so early. The proportions of the house are compatible with a mid-eighteenth century date. The details of windows, doors, and colossal portico are Greek Revival, however, and probably date from the acquisition of the house by Captain Thomas Lavender in 1842.

None of the other Georgian farmhouses in the Princeton area was conceived on the grand scale of Morven with its balanced wings and formal gardens. Most of them, planned far more casually, began as simple dwellings of one or two rooms with loft above. With growing prosperity, their owners added a larger block, usually of four to eight rooms. Still further additions might be made at a later date, in the form of another wing balancing the earliest construction, or the conversion of a three-bay to a five-bay house.

22. Maybury Hill, Snowden Lane, was advertised for sale in the *New York Gazette or the Weekly Post Boy* of December 24, 1753, by the estate of Aaron Hewes, a mason, who may have built the house as early as 1732 when he sold another property in the western part of Princeton. Its original appearance must have been quite different, for it is described as a good stone house 30 feet square with adjoining stone kitchen. Presumably it then resembled such a vernacular house as the one at 487 Stockton Street (Fig. 10). Its wings were united behind a Georgian façade by a subsequent owner, probably Richard (Derrick) Longstreet, who purchased the property in 1768. Aaron Hewes' son, Joseph Worth Hewes, who was born here, became a Signer of the Declaration of Independence for North Carolina. Although the name has long been applied to this house, the eighteenth-century "Mayberry Hill" was actually an adjoining property belonging to Thomas Leonard.

23. Constitution Hill derived its name from the tradition that the State Constitution of New Jersey was drafted here in 1776. The property was willed to Robert Stockton by his father Richard in 1709 and then passed to his son, the second Robert, Quartermaster during the Revolution. It is difficult to determine when the house was built, but it was probably prior to 1750. It was transitional in type, combining the vertical silhouette, unpretentious use of materials and lack of decoration of early building modes with the high basement and segmental arched windows of the Early Georgian period. By the late nineteenth century it had become a tenant farm. It was demolished in 1896.

24. Mansgrove. This tract was part of the vast holdings of Thomas Leonard in the early eighteenth century. Leonard, who himself lived on his estate known as Grove Hall, leased Mansgrove in 1753 to John Denniston and Patrick Barber. The lease was reassigned to Leonard in 1763 and he offered the property for sale on October 27 of that year. The kitchen wing is undoubtedly the original house, appropriate in scale for a mid-eighteenth century tenant farm; the main wing, with its delicate Federal detailing, was probably added c. 1800.

25. Olden Manor. Now the official residence of the Director of the Institute for Advanced Study, this is the site of the homestead farm of the Olden family. The western wing with its small rooms and low ceilings probably incorporates the house of William Olden, who moved to Stony Brook in 1697. In the late eighteenth century the middle section was added; the east end dates from the mid-nineteenth century.

26. Gulick-Hodge-Scott House, Herrontown Road. The wooden western wing, containing several small low-ceilinged rooms and a separate staircase, has been much altered. However, it still retains its enormous fireplace and bake oven, with its masonry exposed on the side wall, as well as some rough-hewn beams. While its fenestration has been changed several times, probably first to conform to its more grandiose brick addition, its basic ground-hugging silhouette and lack of formal planning would indicate a pre-Revolutionary date. The brick portion of the house is altogether different in spirit. Commodious, elegant and formal, it proclaims both a more affluent way of life and a greater consciousness of aesthetic values. In general outline the brick section resembles a Georgian house. However, the large windows and the delicacy of individual details suggest an early nineteenth-century date. On the exterior the refined and sensitive handling of keyed lintels, cornice, and doorway with its leaded fanlight reveal the hand of a skilled builder familiar with Adamesque motifs. So too does the interior woodwork, particularly that of the parlor mantel, the hallway arch, and the graceful heart-and-tendril step ends. When Major John Gulick died intestate in 1828, the large property he had assembled in 1797 was divided among his surviving children. The land on which this house stands went to his son Isaac. Since several houses of similar style were built on the Gulick property and since the inventory of John Gulick's estate shows that each of his three sons was in his debt for between two and three thousand dollars (a substantial sum in the early nineteenth century), it may be assumed that Isaac Gulick's house antedates his father's death. Certainly the style of the brick section seems consonant with a date of 1800-1820. Later owners of the house included Professor Charles Hodge of the Theological Seminary and General Hugh Lenox Scott, who added the somewhat awkward eastern wing early in the twentieth century.

27. Greenland-Brinson-Gulick House, Princeton-Kingston Road. The small central section of this house, now largely hidden behind a Victorian bay window, was quite possibly built by Henry Greenland, who occupied the land on which it stands sometime before 1685. In its original state it was a one-and-a-half story house with clay-filled walls. Its basement floor is earth; large boulders, not exacavated, but incorporated directly into the foundations, are still visible. The property passed from Greenland to his son-in-law Daniel Brinson and thence to Daniel's son, Barefoot Brinson. It was advertised for sale after the latter's death in 1748. The building was undoubtedly enlarged during the Brinson ownership by the addition of a two-story wing to the west, the roof of the original house being raised to conform to the new height, and the whole clapboarded. The paneled fireplace wall of the center room (which John Gulick referred to as the "family room") with its in-wall staircase is of an early eighteenth-century type and must date from this first renovation. A further major addition, the taller wing to the east, was made by John Gulick, following his purchase of the property in 1797. Despite the somewhat false impression created by the Victorian roof and cornice, this is a Federal structure, so close in detail to the house across the way at 1091 Princeton-Kingston Road and to the Gulick-Hodge-Scott House that they may be assumed to be by the same hand. The mill property across the road has always been closely associated with this house. Originally in common ownership, the former was sold separately by Barefoot Brinson's heirs. It passed through several hands, including those of the Skillman family and Ezekiel Forman, who called it New Market. During the Revolution the mills, then belonging to Lemuel Scudder, whose brother owned the Aqueduct Mills at the juncture of Stony Brook and the Millstone River, were destroyed by the British. The properties were reunited in the Gulick purchase.

28. Detail, doorway, Gulick-Hodge-Scott House.
The elegance and the refined attenuation of classic detail are characteristic of Federal architecture.

29. Detail, doorway, 1091 Princeton-Kingston Road.

30. Prospect. Watercolor by Maria Templeton, 1797. This pre-Revolutionary frame house stood on the site now occupied by the residence of the President of Princeton University. (It was demolished and the present stone villa, designed by John Notman, built in 1849.) Prior to the Revolution the house was owned by Jonathan Baldwin. In 1779 Colonel George Morgan purchased the property and proceeded to improve the house, outbuildings, and grounds in accord with the era's most advanced ideas of scientific agriculture. His modernization of the house undoubtedly included the addition of dormers and a pedimented doorway. He probably also replaced earlier casement windows or small-paned sash with the larger panes which came into favor after the Revolution, for in 1783 he paid Philip Hartman for one hundred and ten sash lights. His account books and those of his son, John, who operated the property from 1796 to 1805, show that no farmer could devote his resources solely to his residence. A farm was a complex of buildings, with the barns often dominant in size and importance over the house. Separate kitchen, smokehouse, icehouse, "barracks" for grain storage, and other outbuildings all required attention. Careful consideration of functional requirements, simple but pleasing proportions, and sound construction and craftsmanship often made of these outbuildings minor works of art.

31. Castle Howard, Smokehouse.

Few outbuildings survive. Those that do are reminders of the many anonymous craftsmen essential to eighteenth-century building; the mason to set the stone; the carpenter to put together a door; the blacksmith to forge the massive strap hinges and latches. The probable builder of the barn at Maybury Hill is known, however. Aaron Hewes, who purchased the property around 1735, was a mason, and the barn is testimony to his skill.

32. Maybury Hill, Barn.

33. Morven, "Slave Quarters." The original use of the small house behind Morven's east wing is unknown. It may have been a tenant house when the property belonged to John Stockton, or a "bride's house" erected by Richard Stockton the Signer while Morven was being built. Like Morven it has been much altered; the remaining twelve-over-eight windows, similar to those at the Quaker Meeting House, suggest a mid-eighteenth century date.

34. Tusculum, Barn. This handsome stone barn was probably built in the early nineteenth century. More formal than the barn at Maybury Hill, with symmetrically placed windows and doors, it uses the elliptical arches popular in the four decades following the Revolution.

A North-West Prospect of Nassau-Hall, with a Front View of the Presidents House in New Jersey.

35. Nassau Hall in 1764, drawn by W. Tennent and engraved by H. Dawkins. This, the most comprehensive eighteenth-century view of the college, shows not only Nassau Hall and the President's House but a group of small dwellings to the east. These include the steward's house directly left of Nassau Hall as well as part of the four lots and three houses advertised for sale in the *Pennsylvania Journal* of June 30, 1763. They are described as adjoining the college to the west and the land of George Campbell (keeper of the Hudibras) to the north, and being all post-and-rail fenced. Although the principal college buildings were completed by 1757, the Trustees continued to add embellishments, however sparse, to the grounds. In 1760 they commissioned Robert Smith to build the "pale fence"

shown around the President's House. The fence in front of Nassau Hall was evidently a conceit of the artist. In 1770 and 1771 brick was purchased (from Joshua Anderson and Joseph Hornor) for paving the walks and for the "College Wall." The latter surrounded Nassau Hall's forecourt when Moreau de St. Méry visited Princeton in 1794. Still the college remained stark and austere, rising from a barren field, but it impressed most viewers. Although that sophisticated Frenchman, the Marquis de Chastellux, described it as remarkable for nothing but its size, his younger fellow officers considered the building beautiful or handsome. Many observers commented on its hilltop site, dominating the countryside as the college had come to dominate the town.

III · THE COLLEGE BUILDS

HE earliest colleges in the New World owed their existence to the church. Harvard and Yale were founded by Congregationalists, William and Mary and Columbia by Anglicans, Rutgers by Dutch Reformed, and Brown by Baptists. The secularization of these institutions took place only much later. It is within this religious context that we must look for the beginnings of the future College of New Jersey.

A great religious revival swept through the Colonies in the 1740's and 1750's, spurred by a group of evangelists who emphasized the importance of personal religious experience in their fervent pleas for reform within the church. The Great Awakening, for so it was called by contemporaries, caused a serious and for a time unresolvable conflict within the Presbyterian Church, arising over education for the ministry. The zealots, the New Lights, insisted that the conventional education in established colleges advocated by the Old Side conservatives was producing neither the quantity nor the proper kind of ministers needed. A number of New Light ministers, including Jonathan Dickinson and Aaron Burr, Sr., started their own courses of instruction. The most important of these New Light groups was William Tennent's Log College at Neshaminy, Bucks County, Pennsylvania. Since the New Lights realized that their young men would never be ordained by the Old Side-dominated Philadelphia Synod, they used the New Brunswick Presbytery to ordain them. For this act of defiance the Philadelphia Synod expelled the New Brunswick Presbytery and simultaneously delivered a diatribe against the New Lights. The New York Presbytery, sympathetic to the New Light cause, then left the Philadelphia Synod and together with New Brunswick formed the new Synod of New York.

It was clear to the New Lights that now they must produce significant numbers of ministers to survive the attacks of the Old Side. William Tennent was by this time, 1738, too old to operate the Log College actively, and other New Light ministers were too occupied with their pastoral duties to devote sufficient time to training more than a few young men.

A solution was devised by four eminent clergymen, Jonathan Dickinson, Aaron Burr, Sr., Ebenezer Pemberton, and John Pierson, who decided to found a college in which to educate ministers for their New Light brand of religion. After securing the active support of three prominent New York laymen these founders set out to organize the new college.

To gain approval from the King and the Anglican Governor of New Jersey for a charter, they decided to propose a college which would admit all denominations and include laymen as well as candidates for the ministry. The college was to be of a high level, equal to that of Harvard or Yale. In 1745 Governor Lewis Morris of New Jersey, not convinced of the popularity of the proposed new college among Quakers and Anglicans, refused to grant a charter. But in May 1746 Morris died. His aged

43

successor, Governor John Hamilton, under the influence of his advisors, signed the charter on October 22, 1746. In 1747 Jonathan Belcher, a Congregationalist from Massachusetts, became Governor of the Province. Wearied by the narrow-minded conservatism at Harvard and Yale, Belcher gave his wholehearted support to the new college. To repulse continued attacks about the legality of the college's charter, Belcher issued a new and sounder one.

Jonathan Dickinson, the tireless leader of the New York Synod, became the first president of the college, which opened with a handful of students in Elizabeth, New Jersey, in May 1747. Very shortly he died and was succeeded by Aaron Burr, Sr., also a distinguished scholar and theologian. From the autumn of 1747 until 1756, when the college found its permanent home, the students lived and worked in Newark at Burr's parsonage.

Strenuous efforts were made to raise funds through lotteries in the Colonies and through direct appeals to dissenters in England and Scotland. Meanwhile the trustees were busy making plans to spend the money and debating where the college should settle. Although Newark and Elizabeth both wanted it, Governor Belcher and the interested Philadelphians fought for a more central location between New York and Philadelphia. The choice finally narrowed to New Brunswick or Princeton, with the stipulation that there should be provided ten acres of clear land, two hundred acres of woodland for fuel, and a thousand pounds of New Jersey currency.

At the trustees' meeting on January 24, 1753, a group of townsmen from Princeton unexpectedly announced that it had fulfilled all the requirements. At this time Burr had in his possession a preliminary plan of a proposed building. The author of this plan is unknown. We do know from some of Burr's correspondence that a local stone mason, William Worth, was involved in the planning of the new building. At the trustees' meeting on July 22, 1754, a building committee was appointed and the final plan for the building approved. It was decided that "... laying the Foundation of the College be proceeded upon immediately. That the Plan drawn by Doct^r. Shippen & Mr Robert Smith be in general the Plan of the College. That the College be built of Brick if good Brick can be made at Princeton & if Sand can be got reasonably cheap—That it be three Story high & without any Cellar." The plan is preserved only in a printed version of the diary of Ezra Stiles, future eighth president of Yale.

Robert Smith was a carpenter-builder from Philadelphia who had worked on the Second Presbyterian Church, Philadelphia (of which several trustees were members), and the steeple of Christ Church, Philadelphia, and was later to design Carpenters' Hall in the same city. Dr. William Shippen, a Philadelphia physician, was a brother of Edward Shippen, a college trustee.

Only a week after the trustees voted to accept the Smith-Shippen plan, ground was broken. On August 5th President Burr wrote about "Mr. Worth's Proposals" which he liked very much. Although we do not know what these proposals were, we can surmise that since Worth was a stone mason they concerned the choice of material to be used. No doubt the trustees were influenced in following Worth's suggestion of using stone by a desire to economize. Thus the final appearance of the building preserved Robert Smith's design but adhered to a local preference for stone. On September 17, 1754, the cornerstone was laid at a brief ceremony recorded by Nathaniel FitzRandolph.

Nassau Hall (Fig. 35) was named for William III, Prince of Orange-Nassau, at the request of Governor Belcher, who had refused to have his own name affixed to it. President Burr said, "We do everything in the plainest and cheapest manner, as far as is consistent with Decency & Convenience, having no superfluous Ornaments." Before successive alterations all but obliterated any traces of Smith's work it was, indeed, a building done in the plainest style. With its high English basement, regular fenestration, low-pitched roof, symmetrical floor plan, and rectangular shape it conformed to Georgian principles, but ornament was kept to the bare minimum. A pediment accentuated the central doorway, a circular window further emphasized this, and a cupola crowned the whole. However the use of local stone gave the building a rustic appearance, related it intimately to its locale, and eliminated the contrast of formal elements that would have been obtained with brick and wood. Thus in plan and elevation the building belonged to the Georgian period; but in material and execution, like the Quaker Meeting House, it harked back to an earlier era.

Specific details used in the design of Nassau Hall can be traced to the usual carpenter's handbooks in circulation at the time: the cupola could have been adapted from one of James Gibbs' designs for English churches. There is however no specific English prototype for the building. Gibbs' design for the Fellows' House at King's College, Cambridge, often mentioned in this connection, is a much more sophisticated building and is notable more for its differences from Nassau Hall than its similarities to it.

In spite of its provincial, homespun look, Nassau Hall, one of the largest public buildings in the colonies, served as a model for many others. It inspired, among others, Hollis Hall, Harvard (1762-63), University Hall, Brown (1773), Dartmouth Hall, Dartmouth (1790), Queen's, Rutgers (1811), and Alexander Hall, Princeton Theological Seminary (1815). Robert Smith even found that its basic design, when adapted, suited his plan for the Walnut Street Jail in Philadelphia (1773-75).

In September 1754 after plans were well under way for the erection of Nassau Hall, the trustees decided to build a house for the President (Fig. 36), to be constructed of wood and designed by Robert Smith. This time, perhaps in deference to Smith's preference for brick, the trustees allowed a measure of elegance and switched from wood to brick. Although a few additions and alterations have been made over the years, the house today is essentially the one that Robert Smith built for President Burr, who died in 1757 only a few months after the house was finished.

The same principles of Georgian design underlie both Morven and the President's House (now called the Dean's House). Less ambitious than Morven, it is impressive for its eloquent simplicity and quiet refinement. It seems eminently suitable for housing the sober, religious, devoted scholar and teacher that Burr must have been. Like Philadelphia houses of the period, the President's House reserves its elegance for the interior. Though subdued in comparison to the exuberant decorative details of Virginian Georgian houses, the finely executed woodwork of the President's House deserves admiration. From this house, rather than from Nassau Hall, we understand why Robert Smith was so highly regarded as an architect by his contemporaries.

36. The Dean's House. Occupied by all presidents of the college from 1756 until 1879, it then became the official residence of the Dean of the Faculty. The roof has been raised and pierced by a dormer; the bay window on the east wall and a cast-iron porch were added in 1868 (the latter replaced by the present porch c. 1905); the handsome cast-iron fence was erected in 1852. The alterations have been relatively minor, however, and the Dean's house is far more faithful to Robert Smith's original conception than is the much-remodeled Nassau Hall.

37. Nassau Hall, south wall of the west wing. Tradition claims that a cannonball, fired by an American artillery battery under the command of Alexander Hamilton, struck the wall during the Battle of Princeton in January 1777. The scar is said to be in the midst of the patch of ivy between the two windows at the lower right.

IV · THE REVOLUTION

THE young College of New Jersey did not remain for long in tranquil possession of its new facilities. Within two decades it became involved in activities that disrupted its functions for years, scattered or incapacitated its students, faculty, and trustees, and nearly ruined its buildings.

As the colonials' dissatisfaction with British handling of their affairs grew, so did patriotic fervor on the Princeton campus. Commencement speeches became harangues on the benefits of liberty and freedom and the superior virtues of American manufactures. To show its patriotism the entire class of 1771 wore American cloth at Commencement. Less symbolic but more direct action was taken with the interception of a letter from the merchants of New York to those of Philadelphia, informing the latter of their decision to break the non-importation agreement. The students seized the letter and, in black-gowned procession, burnt it, to the tolling of the college bell. The college's supply of tea was burned with similar ceremony in January 1774. Undoubtedly the students were heartily supported by John Witherspoon, the fiery Scottish divine who had accepted the presidency of the college in 1768. Despite the heavy burr that in moments of excitement made his speech almost unintelligible, he had rapidly become a thorough-going American and an effective spokesman for the patriot cause. With college trustee Richard Stockton, he became a member of the Continental Congress and a signer of the Declaration of Independence; its proclamation was celebrated in Princeton on July 9, 1776, by an illumination of Nassau Hall. Within six months the building would be in the hands of the British.

In the late fall and winter of 1776, Washington fled across New Jersey. Repeatedly his capture seemed inevitable, but a series of British miscalculations and delays allowed his escape. As the Continental Army approached Princeton, the inhabitants prepared for invasion. At Morven, Richard Stockton hid the family silver and fled with his wife and all but one of his children to Monmouth County, only to fall into the hands of the British there. John Witherspoon regretfully disbanded his college and, like most of his students, left town. The aged and anonymous farmer who wrote, "A Breif Narrative of the Ravages committed by the Regular and Hessian Soldiers . . ." commented, "Most of the Inhabitants of Prince Town . . . left their Dwelling Houses and went where they could go with their Familys . . . and left a Great Part of their goods behind them in their houses for want of Carriages to take them. . . ."

Stopping only briefly at Princeton, Washington hastened to cross the Delaware at Trenton. Once again the British hesitated at the river bank. On December 12 General Sir William Howe ordered his Army into winter quarters, leaving a thin chain of troops spread through the Jerseys. Washington was still in a difficult, almost desperate, position. Desertion, disease, and lack of adequate supplies had reduced his effective fighting force to a dispirited handful. Hoped-for reinforcements were slow in arriving. In

New Jersey and Pennsylvania, Loyalists came out in the open; waverers hastened to sign General Howe's protection papers; Congress, fearing the imminent loss of Philadelphia, fled to Baltimore.

Washington, however, had no intention of giving way to despair. Instead he began to plan a bold strike. On Christmas night, 1776, in the extreme winds and biting cold of a vicious northeaster, he crossed the Delaware at McKonkey's Ferry and marched swiftly over the icy roads to Trenton. There the Hessian garrison, worn out after a boisterous Christmas celebration, was completely surprised. The battle was swift and one-sided. The majority of the Hessians, some nine hundred officers and men, and most of their artillery were captured and taken back to Pennsylvania.

Within a few days Washington, encouraged by the reenlistment of most of his regulars and by intelligence reports of panic among the British, decided to make another attempt to regain control of central New Jersey. On December 31 the American Army returned to Trenton. Under the command of Cornwallis, who had been hastily summoned from New York where he had been about to embark for England, the British advanced to meet them. They reached Trenton on January 2, and the two armies met in brief and inconclusive engagements late in the afternoon. Once again Cornwallis chose to delay, planning to wait until daylight to mount a general attack. But on the morrow the Continental army was no longer there. Leaving their campfires burning, they had proceeded, with muffled gun carriages, along a back road to Princeton. Their route, sketched for them by Cadwalader from information received from "a very intelligent young gentleman," is preserved in the so-called spy map now in the Library of Congress.

At daybreak the American troops reached the wood lot of the Quaker Meeting House and wheeled right along the back road. A small detachment under General Hugh Mercer was sent forward along the Quaker Bridge Road to destroy the bridge over Stony Brook. At the same time, the British garrison at Princeton, under Colonel Charles Mawhood, was marching south on the Lawrenceville Road to join Cornwallis at Trenton. As the vanguard climbed the hill beyond Worth's Mill they observed the movement of the Americans. Reversing their march they came back along the road and then cut across the fields toward high ground. Mercer, apprised of their presence, turned to the right and encountered them in William Clark's orchard. In a brief, but vicious, seesaw battle, joined finally by troops from the main American column, the British were routed. The victorious Americans marched on to take the town. Too exhausted to attempt the capture of their chief objective, the main British supply depot and treasury at New Brunswick, they turned north at Kingston and headed for winter quarters at Morristown.

The significance of Washington's victory at Princeton escaped neither the participants nor later commentators. As soon as the battle ended, Washington and some of his men appeared at the Thomas Olden house, requesting aid for the wounded.

". . . Though they were both hungry and thirsty some of them laughing out right, others smileing, and not a man among them but showed Joy in his Countenance." Frederick the Great described the campaign of Trenton and Princeton as the ". . . most brilliant recorded in the annals of military achievements." And Cornwallis, toasting Washington after the surrender at Yorktown said, ". . . fame will gather your brightest laurels rather from the banks of the Delaware than from those of the Chesapeake." Indeed the accomplishments had been formidable. Washington had proved his ability to meet and, by a series of canny maneuvers, best the finest troops the British could put in the field. His abilities to command were never seriously doubted again. Confidence in the possibility of eventual success rose throughout the Colonies. Of most immediate benefit was the rise in the rate of enlistments and in the support given to the army by the population of New Jersey. Thus reinforced, Washington was able to maintain control of most of the State. Perhaps the behavior of the British troops in the Jerseys was as responsible as Washington's victories for the conversion of many waverers to the patriot cause. One observer, commenting on the British occupation, wrote, ". . . that where Congress had made one whig, General Howe had made ten. . . ."

Indeed Princeton had suffered greatly. One participant in the battle noted, "This is a very pretty little town . . . the houses are built of brick and are very elegant especially the College . . . but the whole town has been ravaged and ruined by the enemy." Ignoring Howe's protection papers and the commands of their own officers, the soldiers plundered the property of patriots, neutrals, and Tories indiscriminately. Christopher Beekman, a tavernkeeper, who must have been one of Princeton's fashion plates, reported the loss, among other items, of buckskin breeches with silver buttons, an assortment of coats and jackets, two hats, ten shirts, and a pair of shoes. Other losses were far more serious. Jonathan Sergeant's new house, on the present site of the Nassau Club, was burned to the ground and the garden destroyed. He estimated their value at £620.1.8. Quartermaster Robert Stockton's house at Constitution Hill was spared, but he filed claims for losses and damages to furnishings, equipment, and produce worth over £655. Tusculum, John Witherspoon's farm, was used to quarter British troops, but was evidently not pillaged, for no claims for damages were filed.

The greatest losses were those incurred by Richard Stockton and the college. Although there seems to be no foundation for the legend that a part of Morven (which was used as headquarters by both Colonel Harcourt and General Cornwallis) was burned, its contents—furnishings, clothing, paintings, books, and papers—were destroyed or stolen. The livestock and the winter's feed supply were also taken. Benjamin Rush, Stockton's son-in-law, who was present at the battle of Princeton, estimated the losses as not less than £5000. Nassau Hall, the object of an artillery attack during the battle, suffered more from its several years' occupancy as barracks and hospital than it did from the bombardment. The college library was sacked and the delicate mechanism of the Rittenhouse orrery wrecked. Although John Witherspoon resumed instruction at the President's House in the summer of 1777, he found that "attendance was difficult and uncertain," and even when the college regained use of Nassau Hall the following summer it was ". . . in so ruinous a state as to be very unfit for accommodating the scholars. . . ." Indeed, despite numerous patchy repairs, the building remained in bad condition until a major restoration was undertaken in the early nineteenth century.

Despite its physical condition, Nassau Hall probably never housed a more glittering assembly in its library and prayer hall than during late June to early November 1783. Congress, threatened by mutinous soldiers in Philadelphia, had hastily fled to the relative safety of rural New Jersey. Its distinguished members were quartered, often none too comfortably, in taverns and the homes of local residents. Elias Boudinot, President of Congress, resided with his sister, Annis Stockton, at Morven. Washington arrived in August and took occupancy of Rockingham, the home of John Berrien's widow at Rocky Hill. The press of business and the summer heat did not preclude a convivial social season. Washington sent to New York for a cook skilled in preparing for and serving a large company. The Boudinot-Stockton household was also lavish in dispensing hospitality. Princeton's purveyors of foodstuffs, accommodating themselves to the visitors' more sophisticated palates, imported such delicacies as pineapples, oranges, and lemons from the Philadelphia market.

The debates in Nassau Hall were not particularly productive. They centered on three issues: disbanding the army, establishing a peacetime military force, and choosing a permanent site for the seat of the government. Only the first of these was resolved with any degree of success. While its inconclusiveness was probably frustrating to the delegates, the session did witness events and ceremonies which must have brought them ample satisfaction. On August 26, Washington rode to Nassau Hall to receive and acknowledge the official thanks of Congress. In October, although the war was not yet officially concluded, he penned his Farewell Orders to the Army in the Blue Room at Rockingham (Fig. 44). On October 31, Pieter Johannes van Berckel, the newly-arrived Dutch Minister, representative of the first nation other than France to recognize the new country, presented his credentials to Congress. That same day word was received of the signing of the peace treaty.

These were stirring events, although Boudinot felt himself "greatly mortified" that Congress' location in a "small Country village" precluded their celebration with proper ceremony. His sentiments were not unique. Other members of Congress felt themselves inconvenienced by the town's inadequate facilities and cramped accommodations. Princeton's brief tenure as the nation's capital was drawing to a close. Following the adjournment of Congress on November 4, its members left Princeton with few regrets and no intention of returning.

38. The Bridge over Stony Brook, Stockton Street at the Quaker Bridge Road. As Washington approached Princeton on the morning of January 3, 1777, he ordered a detachment under General Hugh Mercer to remove the wooden bridge which then spanned Stony Brook. En route Mercer sighted British troops on the hill beyond the bridge. Both forces turned towards the east, meeting near what is now Mercer Road. After the engagement, the bridge was destroyed. It was replaced by the present span in 1792.

39. Detail, Portrait of George Washington by Charles Willson Peale, 1784. In the summer of 1783, while Congress met at Princeton, the college trustees commissioned this painting. Peale showed Washington against the background of the Battle of Princeton. Here, with a touch of artistic license, the victorious Americans are shown pursuing the fleeing British before the south façade of Nassau Hall.

40. Princeton as seen from the Battlefield. Pencil sketch by
John Trumbull, dated Dec. 10, 1790. The heroic aspects of the
Battle of Princeton engaged Trumbull's attention as a recurring
theme from 1786 until shortly before his death in 1843. In 1790
he visited Princeton to sketch the actual terrain. Like most
renditions of the battlefield, this shows few trees. Instead,
cleared fields stretch almost as far as the eye can see, with
Nassau Hall (left of center) and Prospect (far right) plainly
visible on their distant ridge. The small tree in the center is
probably the Mercer Oak, still standing on the battlefield, under
which the wounded General is said to have been laid by his men.

41. (Overleaf) The Battle of Princeton. Painting by James
Peale. Peale has summarized the action in William Clarke's
orchard in which the British first overwhelmed Mercer's small
detachment, only to be routed in turn by troops from the main
Continental column. Although it has been suggested that the
buildings in the background are those of the extant Thomas
Clarke farm, the disposition of the troops indicate rather that
they represent the William Clarke farm. Its buildings have long
since disappeared; the approximate site of the farmhouse is
now marked by a pyramid of shot. In any event, the William
Clarke house must have been much like Thomas Clarke's house,
a rambling construction, built in three sections, with the tall,
narrow proportions so prevalent in the English settlements
along the Delaware. Its outbuildings, however, were of Dutch
derivation. Taken together, house and barns are symbolic of
the intermingling of the two cultures in eighteenth-century
New Jersey.

41

42. Thomas Clarke House. To this farm, described as a new house at the time of the Revolution, General Mercer was carried from the battlefield. Despite careful nursing by its Quaker occupants, he died of his wounds here. The house faced the back road used by Washington's troops, which is no longer in existence; the battlefield is at its back.

43 and 44. Rockingham, as it looked before restoration and today. The older part of this house, the dining room and "Blue Room," was built in 1734; an enlargement c. 1760 transformed it into a Georgian farmhouse influenced by New England types. During the Princeton session of the Continental Congress in 1783 it was rented from the widow of Judge John Berrien as headquarters for Washington. In succeeding years the house fell into disrepair, finally serving as a boardinghouse for workers in a neighboring quarry. Twice moved, and restored to an approximation of its appearance during Washington's occupancy, it is now the property of the State of New Jersey.

45. South side of Nassau Street east of Washington Road. By the end of the eighteenth century Princeton had grown to a small village of about a hundred houses. Most stood lining Nassau Street, set close to the road and to one another, with gardens stretching behind them. Those built after the middle of the eighteenth century were generally raised on a high basement and approached by a short flight of steps. Although row houses were not built in Princeton, the placing of houses in relation to one another and to the street made for a surprisingly urban effect.

V · THE TOWN

In the Eighteenth and Early Nineteenth Centuries

THE comments of the steadily increasing numbers of European observers who braved the discomforts of the crude road across New Jersey provide a valuable record of the changes in the countryside along the route. In the forty-six years between Peter Kalm's visit and Moreau de Saint Méry's in 1794, Princeton had changed from a sparsely populated farming hamlet to a bustling although still small country town. Kalm noticed the well-cultivated fields; Moreau de Saint Méry was impressed by the resemblance of Princeton to the towns through which he had just passed outside of Philadelphia. Princeton, he said, consisted of about eighty houses lining the road, nearly all built of brick. Like the Delaware River towns of Burlington and Trenton, Princeton owed its inception and early growth to its location along a transportation artery. The disposition of houses along a river or road, a typical pattern found in these transportation towns, contrasts with the characteristic New England organization of a town around the green.

In the late seventeenth century one had the choice on the journey from the Raritan River to the Falls of the Delaware of one of two Indian trails, either through Rocky Hill or through Princeton. By the eighteenth century, travelers, warned of the arduous climb up Rocky Hill, preferred the easier Princeton route. The earliest paths were just wide enough for a man and a pack horse to pass. Traffic increased so much that by 1716 the Colonial Assembly ordered that roads be four rods wide, that surveyors be appointed in each town, and that Justices of the Peace commandeer townspeople to construct the roads (a process that consisted only in cutting back the trees from the trails to the desired width). In the middle of the eighteenth century the growth of Princeton and the arrival of the college necessitated an additional road (now Witherspoon Street) beginning opposite the college and joining the route to Rocky Hill and Somerset Court House (now Millstone).

Until 1766 it took three days for a stagecoach to make the trip from New York to Philadelphia. In that year, with better roads, the trip was reduced to two days, a feat facilitated by stages from opposite directions meeting in Princeton. Almost midway between New York and Philadelphia, Princeton became a natural overnight stopping place, and the resulting influx of travelers made tavern keeping the most important business in town. A confirmed Yankee from Connecticut, Silas Deane, wrote in 1774, "The town is inferior by much to Colchester for soil, buildings and improvements, but the people are neat, and there is elegant entertainment for strangers at the tavern."

Activity centered in the taverns, some of which existed even before the arrival of the college in 1756. In fact, the first mention we have of a tavern in Princeton is in a newspaper advertisement of 1734. Princeton was already an active market town holding two-day country fairs where livestock and farm products could be exchanged for household wares and other merchandise. The taverns were the only secular public buildings in the town. Here the townspeople met informally to chat and to read the newspaper. Here one could find the only dancing or entertainment in town. Here was held every type of function imaginable from college trustees' dinners, requiring forty bottles of wine, to medical society meetings and fencing classes. For travelers the inns meant rest, food, and entertainment; for their horses, feed and shelter. For the townsman, contact with the outside world was provided through talks with travelers at the inns.

Unfortunately, none of the numerous Princeton hostelries mentioned in eighteenth-century newspaper advertisements is extant. Among the most famous pre-Revolutionary inns were the Hudibras, on the south side of Nassau Street at College Lane, the King's Arms, and the Sign of the College (Nassau Inn), both on the north side of the street. A fourth, located just to the west of the present site of the First Presbyterian Church, predated the college and after the Revolution acquired the name of the Thirteen Stars. Architecturally the taverns contributed nothing new to the history of Princeton. In most cases they were opened in the homes of the proprietors, changing hands from time to time and being enlarged as need arose. Distinguishable only by their signs, they resembled in all other respects eighteenth-century town houses lining the main road. The Hudibras, one of the largest, could accommodate as many as forty guests and thirty horses.

In response to the services required by travelers, townspeople, and the college, shops and professional offices were opened. Physicians, lawyers, shoemakers, silversmiths, watchmakers, cabinet and carriage makers, as well as merchants who sold everything from books to salt and needles, comprised an urban middle class quite different from the landed gentry. Men like Jacob Hyer, hatter, and Elias Boudinot, Sr., silversmith, combined their trades with tavern keeping. In the eighteenth century, as today, some of the college alumni chose to practice their professions or businesses near Nassau Hall. Jonathan Dickinson Sergeant, class of 1762, lawyer and legislator, settled here, as did Absalom Bainbridge, 1762, a physician; Enos Kelsey, 1766, a storekeeper; and Samuel Bayard, 1784, a lawyer.

The shift of activity from farming around Stony Brook to trade along Nassau Street demanded new types of buildings. Most of the shops and houses built by the new middle class must have been modest; in 1758 a petition to the Provincial General Assembly at Burlington for a barracks cited the hardship of quartering soldiers since ". . . many of your petitioners are poor, have small houses, and numerous families with not more than one room. . . ." Even though the townfolk may have exaggerated their plight to impress the legislators, there is little doubt that many eighteenth-century houses were small. None of these shopkeepers' houses remains in its original state. Some survive as smaller wings attached to larger, more impressive nineteenth-century buildings, only their lower ceilings and smaller proportions revealing their humble eighteenth-century origins. These simple shopkeepers' houses differed little from their seventeenth-century predecessors except that they now had sliding sash windows, perhaps larger and more symmetrically placed, and lower-pitched roofs. In nineteenth-century enlargements of these houses the earlier wing usually came to serve as the kitchen, the later section containing the parlor and more formal rooms.

Although many of the shopkeepers' houses were as small as one or two rooms, the average town house contained five or six rooms and some were as large as eight or ten rooms. Well-to-do townsmen built commodious handsome homes which were the urban counterpart of those of the country gentry, modeled after prototypes in New York and Philadelphia. Provincial and conservative in comparison to Philadelphia Georgian mansions, Princeton's houses nevertheless reflected the confidence that men of the eighteenth century felt in their ability to understand and control the material world. In one century these colonists had converted an uninhabited land of forests into a civilized society of farms and towns. Classical architecture based on order and clarity was the tangible expression of their successful struggle with nature.

Of the handful of large eighteenth-century townhouses that remain in Princeton, the earliest is the President's House (Fig. 49, now the residence of the Dean of the Faculty), built about 1754-55. Two others, Bainbridge House (Fig. 48) and Beatty House (Fig. 50), are particularly representative of two phases in the development of the local Georgian style. If not as impressive in scale or setting as Morven, they rival it in formality and elegance. Like Morven, they were designed not by professional architects but by gentlemen amateurs and skilled artisans who used the ubiquitous English pattern books of the day to guide them. American builders adapted and in most cases simplified the exuberant Baroque designs of the English Georgian into a flatter yet even clearer ordering of the design elements. This is particularly true of Princeton's Georgian houses, which never exhibit anything but the utmost restraint and simplicity. Both Bainbridge House and Beatty House conform to precepts of axial symmetry, closed rectangular shape, and classical decorative vocabulary.

Bainbridge House (Fig. 48) betrays its earlier date in its heaviness of detail, simplicity of design, and contrasts of colors and texture. These contrasts, so vigorous in the original state of the façade in which wooden trim of windows, door, and cornice was set off against unpainted brick laid in Flemish bond, are today obliterated. The symmetry of the façade, the triangular pediment over the doorway, and the molded water table are all typical of the American Early Georgian style of mid-century. The heavy, masculine, straightforwardness of this style is expressed in Bainbridge House by the use of the large broad-keyed lintels over the windows and the bold modillion cornice which sits heavily on the second story windows, cutting their lintels to only half the height of those below. Originally, the sturdy paneled shutters and twelve-over-twelve paned windows of the ground floor gave way to louvered shutters and twelve-over-eight paned windows above, thus effecting a diminution of scale from ground to roof-line. The floor plan of Bainbridge House is a typical one of the period. Floor-to-ceiling paneling remains in the main chamber on the second floor, and one of the corner fireplaces, surrounded by simple floor-to-ceiling paneling, exists in a state approximating the original.

Built in the late 1780's or early '90's, Beatty House (Fig. 50) represents the more delicate and complicated interpretation characteristic of the Late Georgian style. The use of wood as the only material eliminates any textural contrast. The flat two-dimensional façade, a diagram of the space inside, expresses its more complex design in the relationship of shapes. The windows, larger than those in Bainbridge House, with keyed lintels, echo but also contrast with the fanlighted front door and round-headed dormers. The vertical axis of the façade is emphasized by the more elaborate doorway and the Palladian window above. But the horizontal axis of the façade is still dominant, for the ratio of the width to the height is far greater than in Bainbridge House. An increasing use of classical decorative detail, flatter, lighter, and smaller in scale, characterized post-Revolutionary architecture in America. In Beatty House this is concentrated in the pedimented dormers, enframed by pilasters, the fine cornice with both modillions and dentils, and the segmental arched doorway. This preference for oval and fanshaped motifs and for reeding and gouging on pilasters and architrave is notable in Middle Colony architecture.

The interior of Beatty House is distinguished by its spacious entrance hall, well-proportioned living, dining, and drawing rooms, and two handsome Adamesque mantels. There is no floor-to-ceiling paneling, only a chair rail, for by the late eighteenth century paneling had given way to smooth plastered walls. Carved mantelpieces thus assumed a much more important function in the decorative scheme as a whole.

Scattered along Nassau Street there are a few other eighteenth-century houses, most of them isolated from their contemporaries. Queenston, however, the area around the intersection of Harrison and Nassau Streets (Figs. 55, 56, 57), is a neighborhood bearing some resemblance to its earlier character of a crossroads settlement. Although many houses in the area have been greatly altered, some look much as they did two hundred years ago when Jugtown (as it was popularly known) was a thriving community with a pottery works, a tannery, and a hotel in addition to its houses.

46. North side of Nassau Street. By the late eighteenth century most visitors were impressed by Princeton's urban appearance, evidently remarkable in a town whose center contained only seventy or eighty houses. Ranked closely on either side of the broad (and muddy or dusty) expanse of Nassau Street, Princeton's houses ranged from simple one- or two-story constructions of stone or wood to elegant three- and four-story brick townhouses. In addition to dwellings and shops there were a brick Presbyterian church of the meetinghouse type, erected between 1762 and 1766, and at least two schools. Samuel Finley announced the opening of a grammar school affiliated with the college in 1764, at which time a "common English School" was already in operation. Eighteenth-century Princeton had changed comparatively little by the time this photograph was taken in the early 1860's. Among the most prominent buildings in the center of town were the several inns that served both visitors to the college and travelers on the stagecoach route between New York and Philadelphia. One of the most famous, variously known as the Nassau Inn, the College Inn, and the Sign of the College (center left), was built prior to 1757. In its long history (it was kept continuously as an inn, although altered many times, until demolished, with its neighbors, to make way for Palmer Square in 1937), the "Nass" was the site of bibulous pre-Revolutionary commencement dinners for the college trustees; of early meetings of the New Jersey Medical Society and committees of the New Jersey Legislature; of public celebrations of the Fourth of July and Bastille Day; of balls, concerts, and circuses; and of convivial evenings for generations of Princeton undergraduates. The building directly to the east is the Mansion House, later incorporated into the Nassau Inn. Although built by Charles Steadman in 1836, its style conforms to that of its eighteenth-century neighbor. Only the unadorned heaviness of its rectangular sills, lintels, and cornice give some clue to its later date.

48. Bainbridge House, 158 Nassau Street. Built c. 1755-60, this was one of several rental properties owned by Robert Stockton of Constitution Hill. William Bainbridge, commander of the U.S.S. *Constitution*, was born here in 1774, during the tenancy of his father, Dr. Absalom Bainbridge. On Robert Stockton's death, the house went to Dr. Ebenezer Stockton, who maintained it as his residence and office for the practice of medicine for about forty years. This photograph was taken in the early 1870's, around the time that the property was purchased from the Stockton family by the college. It demonstrates the clarity and precision with which the elements of the design were originally revealed through the strong contrast of red brick and painted trim. The striking resemblance of Bainbridge House to the Dean's House leads to the assumption that they were executed at approximately the same time. *(Opposite)*

47. 68-70 Nassau Street. Elias Boudinot, Sr., father-in-law of Richard Stockton the Signer and father of the second Elias, future President of the Continental Congress, offered for sale a ten-room house opposite the College in 1761 and again in 1771. It was probably this stone house in which he plied his numerous trades of silversmith, tavern-keeper, and postmaster. One of the few documents still preserved relating to his business affairs is a bill to the estate of Aaron Burr, Sr., citing charges over a four-month period for a silver thimble, mending a clock, postage, and five and three-quarters gallons of rum. In 1787 the tavern was taken by Christopher Beekman, who patriotically named it the Washington Arms. It remained a tavern until well into the nineteenth century, receiving a coat of stucco about 1850. In the third quarter of the nineteenth century the building was converted into shops and apartments; it was torn down in 1937. Few specialized building types existed in the eighteenth century. Only churches and important public buildings like Nassau Hall deviated from the domestic scale. Like Princeton's other taverns, this was no more than a large dwelling, remarkably similar in type to its close contemporaries, the Dean's House and Bainbridge House.

49. The Dean's House. By the early 1860's the roof had been raised and the brick painted, but the porch which now masks the symmetrical façade had not yet been added. (cf. Fig. 36)

50. Beatty House, 19 Vandeventer Avenue. Hageman says that Beatty House was "supposed to be" a hundred years old in 1879, and stylistically c. 1780 is certainly an acceptable date. Motifs such as the elliptical arch of the fanlight and the accompanying sidelights became generally popular only after the Revolution. Although its first owner was Colonel Jacob Hyer, proprietor of the Hudibras, the house perpetuates the name of a subsequent owner, Colonel Erkuries Beatty. He purchased the house in 1816, moving there from the Castle Howard farm; the diary of his several years as owner of the latter is a valuable record of eighteenth-century agricultural practices. A man of intellect and refinement, Beatty undoubtedly embellished his new property to suit his own taste. He probably added the semicircular portico, with its shallow conical roof supported on four columns, that once adorned the front doorway and the handsome parlor mantel, exhibiting a sophistication in design and a refinement in execution that contrasts with the relative crudity of the other ornament. It was a suitable ornament for the dwelling of a former aide to Lafayette, said to have housed the Marquis on a visit to Princeton in 1825. Originally Beatty House stood on Nassau Street, opposite Bainbridge House. Along with one or two of its neighbors it was moved to its present site in 1875 to make way for expansion of the campus. At that time a clapboard wall, pierced by two windows, was extended over the exposed brick chimney base, and a Victorian porch, removed in a recent restoration, was added.

51, 52, 53. Parlor mantelpiece, Beatty House. The rococo delicacy of the brothers Adam had a profound influence on post-Revolutionary architectural detail in the United States. Garlands, putti, and a delightful bucolic scene embellish this mantel. The post-Revolutionary craftsman chose to stress the playful and picturesque aspects of the classical vocabulary rather than the heavier structural elements favored by his Georgian counterpart.

54. Doorway, 205 Nassau Street. Isaac Anderson, a prosperous cabinet-maker and carriage-builder, erected the substantial brick house at the corner of Charlton and Nassau Streets towards the end of the eighteenth century. It was originally a three-bay house, later expanded to five. Subsequent additions and the installation of a shop window have altered its character considerably. The graceful doorway remains. With its weblike lead tracery, generous fanlight, and dainty carved woodwork, it is a fine example of post-Revolutionary decorative detail.

55. 344 Nassau Street. This house stands on a portion of the original Hornor tract and remained in the hands of that family until about 1840. The lower story of the wing is probably the oldest part of the house, dating from the early years of the Princeton settlement. A break in the masonry at the front marks the height of a former porch and possibly also the height of the original one-room stone house, now stuccoed over. On the west wall the placing of the two surviving small windows, with strap-hinged plank shutters, defines the dimensions of a massive fireplace. The main section is brick. Were it not for documentary evidence that this portion of the house was being built or enlarged in 1824, the present appearance of the building and details such as the plain transom and segmental arched windows would suggest a date sixty or more years earlier. In a provincial town like Princeton, however, styles often arrived late and changed slowly. What was long out of vogue in the metropolis might seem perfectly acceptable to the local builder and his client. Thirty or forty years ago the building still possessed a small two-columned portico which would be consonant with the date of 1824. At present, because of considerable alterations to both the exterior and interior, it is impossible to determine whether the 1824 building activity encompassed the construction of the main block or merely the renovation of an existing structure.

56. Queen's Court, 341 Nassau Street. John Harrison kept a
store at this corner towards the end of the eighteenth century.
In the early nineteenth century John C. Schenck occupied the
premises. His estate advertised the property for sale in July
1836, offering outbuildings, a store and storehouse, and a
"brick Dwelling House adjoining." The last, with its plain
rectangular sills and lintels and round-arched door, was probably built c. 1800-1810. Its modern name was affectionately
applied by Princeton undergraduates during its brief tenure by
a girls' school late in the nineteenth century. The young ladies
were preparing for admission to Evelyn College, which occupied the large shingle house at the end of Evelyn Place.
(Planned to become a female adjunct to Princeton, Evelyn
College languished from 1888 to 1897, finally succumbing for
lack of funds.)

57. 342 Nassau Street. A basement beam inscribed 1730 indicates a plausible date for this house, whose verticality and lack of ornament certainly suggest the early eighteenth century. The wing was originally on the opposite side; it was moved to allow for the widening of Harrison Street. 342 Nassau and its neighbors at the intersection, along with the scattering of other early houses in the vicinity, maintain the scale and atmosphere of the small crossroads settlement Queenston originally was.

58. 41 and 35 Harrison Street. These two plain white frame houses have stood on Harrison Street since the early nineteenth century. A neighboring lot was the site of a small Presbyterian Chapel built in 1832 to serve the Queenston community.

59. 304 Nassau Street. Almost obscured behind the three-storied wooden porches added in the mid-nineteenth century, stands a square brick house. It was built by a man named Vanderveer, probably in the third quarter of the eighteenth century. At the end of that century and in the early years of the nineteenth it was occupied by Roger Gerard van Polanen, former Minister from the Netherlands. Clues to its early date are the keystoned lintels of the façade's second-story windows and the handling of the side wall. Wrought-iron S-shaped beam anchors, segmental arched window headings, and the bricked-up remains of an exterior oven remain as evidence of eighteenth-century construction. It is unlikely that brick was used as a facing material in Princeton before 1755 or 1756, although it was in common use in New Jersey and other parts of the colonies from the late seventeenth century. No written records of brick houses in Princeton exist before that date and, had it been readily available, Robert Smith's recommendation of brick as the material for Nassau Hall would undoubtedly have been followed.

60

61

62. 298 Nassau Street. The wing with its small windows and plain doorway may be a survival of the one- to three-room houses common in early eighteenth-century Princeton. The main section of the house, with its columned portico, reveals (like its former neighbor, now moved to 19 Linden Lane) the hand of Charles Steadman. It probably was built in the early 1830's.

60. 325 Nassau Street. The modest scale of this pre-Revolutionary brick double house is probably more typical of eighteenth-century Princeton than other more elegant survivals.

61. 274 Nassau Street. Like more than sixty other Princeton buildings, 274 Nassau has been moved from its original site to its present location. It once stood at the southwest corner of Nassau and Charlton Streets. The triangular lintels and small portico with attenuated columns indicate a date in the early 1820's.

63. 159 Nassau Street. This is one of the few surviving examples of eighteenth-century domestic architecture in downtown Princeton. Unornamented, in comparison to Bainbridge or Beatty House, it is nevertheless an excellent example of a type once common in Princeton and the surrounding countryside. Eschewing the "L"-shaped wings popular in New England, most central New Jersey builders added extensions laterally. This "stringing-out" to the sides, which also occurs in both the Dutch Colonial houses of northern New Jersey and the English-derived brick houses of the southern part of the state, cannot be attributed to any particular national influence. The result, in the Princeton area, is a characteristic silhouette, a house which appears tall and narrow because the total length of the

façade is great in relation to the building's depth. Like many other houses with no hallmarks of high style, 159 Nassau Street is difficult to date precisely. In a stylistic center like Philadelphia the simple doorway with its four-light transom and shouldered architrave would indicate a date before 1750, as would the small-paned sash, twelve-over-twelve in the first story of the central block and twelve-over-eight above. In Princeton, however, such details are no guarantee of an early date, and the very small dentil molding of the cornice and the narrow window muntins seem more characteristic of the post-Revolutionary era. A date prior to 1786 has been suggested for this house; it is probably correct.

64. Archibald Alexander House. In a letter of October 10, 1812, Archibald Alexander, then newly appointed as Professor at the Princeton Theological Seminary, noted, "On the 29th of July I removed my family to this place, where a house was provided for us, not very large or commodious, but the best which could be obtained." Here he held some classes and preached to his students, until a more satisfactory dwelling was provided on the seminary campus. This old photograph shows the house in its original location on Mercer Street, directly to the east of what is now Trinity Church property. It now stands, much altered, at 134 Mercer Street. The similarity in type to 159 Nassau Street is striking.

65. Detail, 159 Nassau Street. Although glass had been blown in the Colonies since their founding, the process, in the eighteenth century, was far from perfect. Window pane prices were high; sizes were small, gradually increasing as the century progressed. Lack of precise control of materials and manufacturing procedures resulted in the irregularities of surface and variations of color typical of old glass. Eighteenth-century handiwork is also visible here in the fine beaded edge with which carpenters often finished their hand-hewn clapboard.

66. Stanhope Hall. The second major building period at the college followed the virtual destruction of Nassau Hall by fire in 1802. Not only was money readily raised for rebuilding Nassau Hall, but sufficient excess funds were available for new construction. Most prominent among the new buildings were Stanhope Hall and its twin on the opposite side of the campus, Philosophical Hall. It seems likely that Benjamin Henry Latrobe, who had been called in as architect for the reconstruction of Nassau Hall, had a hand in their design. The arrangement of two wings flanking a pedimented central pavilion relates to Nassau Hall. There is, however, a greater subtlety in the handling of the masses; and the penetration of the wall surface by doors and windows and the complicated geometry of their relationship suggest the hand of a sophisticated architect working in a mode somewhat different from the formal and regular cadence of the Georgian.

VI · THE COLLEGE AND THE SEMINARY

In the Early Nineteenth Century

THE post-Revolutionary decades were years of growth for the town but perilous times for the college. The students, inspired by the success of the American and French Revolutions, espoused libertarian ideas. They championed individual rights, freedom of thought, and even sometimes atheism, or at least the separation of religion and education. President John Witherspoon might have been able to divert the enthusiasm of the students into constructive channels; but his successors, Samuel Stanhope Smith, Ashbel Green, and James Carnahan, could think of no answer to their rebelliousness except repression, more rigid rules, and larger doses of religion.

The burning of Nassau Hall in 1802 symbolizes the conflicts that nearly destroyed the college. When President Smith saw the conflagration, he proclaimed it the consequence of "vice and irreligion" and rashly claimed that it was the work of student arsonists. The students, more temperately, believed it to be an accident. Consternation over the destruction of Nassau Hall was not restricted to faculty and trustees but reached a wider public. From *An Elegy on Princeton College* written by an anonymous inmate of the state prison in Trenton in 1802, we read,

> Here many a youth, by emulation led,
> Por'd o'er the sacred volumes of the dead—
> Of Patriot-Heroes caught the zealous rage,
> And drank their spirit from the breathing page.
>
> . . .
>
> But see what consternation! hark the sound!
> What sudden tumult fills the village round!
> Wrapt in a blaze the sumptuous mansion falls,
> Leaving no vestige but the tottering walls!
> Wing'd by the wind the smoaky columns rise,
> And bear the dismal tidings round the skies,
> Then flow descending thro' the distant vale,
> To gazing hamlets tell the gloomy tale.
>
> . . .
>
> FAIR EDIFICE! thy desolated wall,
> Thy dreary ruins, tears of sorrow call!
> But may the liberal SONS of JERSEY raise,
> Bright as thy glory . . . lasting as thy praise,
> Another Phoenix-Structure, that shall stand
> The choicest blessing of the ALMIGHTY's hand.

Whatever the cause of the fire, the architectural consequences of the disaster were beneficial. The college was not yet in such straits that money-raising was difficult: enough funds were raised to pay not only for the rebuilding of Nassau Hall but also for erecting Philosophical and Stanhope Halls. Benjamin Henry Latrobe, trained in Europe, the first professional as well as most distinguished architect of the day in America, was hired for the reconstruction. Latrobe had already designed the Bank of Pennsylvania and the city waterworks in Philadelphia and was later to become the architect for the Capitol in Washington. Although the work on Nassau Hall was not a major commission and Latrobe, who received no compensation for his services, was restricted by the existing fabric of the building, he considered the project ". . . among the most gratifying exertions of my art. . . ." The changes Latrobe made, while individually not significant, nevertheless improved the design of the building immeasurably. It is a pity that virtually nothing of his Nassau Hall remains, for it was the best of the building's several states.

A comparison of Robert Smith's Nassau Hall with Latrobe's (Fig. 69) shows the superiority of a professional's design to that of a carpenter-builder. To give more prominence to the central pavilion and thereby reduce the monotonous effect of the over-long wings on either side, Latrobe replaced Smith's oculus in the central pediment with a larger segmental opening and substituted for the flat lintels over the doors triangular pediments to match the main one. The entrance pavilion was further emphasized by the enlarged and elongated cupola raised on a square base. The raising of the roof line by about two feet eliminated the cramped feeling of Smith's building, where the cornice had rested directly on the lintels of the top story windows, a favorite device of the Georgian carpenter-builder. In sum, Latrobe's improvements produced a more unified building by subordinating its individual parts as much as possible to the total design, which was then focused on the central axis. In these subtle changes made to an existing building, Latrobe showed himself a resourceful, sophisticated architect.

In 1804-1805 Philosophical Hall (demolished in 1873) and Stanhope Hall (Fig. 66) were built flanking Nassau Hall, as part of a symmetrical plan for the campus reinforcing and complementing the classicism and symmetry of the buildings. This scheme (also involving the construction of a Vice-President's house and professors' residences behind Nassau Hall) effected the integration of individual structures, both old and new, into a total building complex. It was, for America, a new concept.

Stanhope Hall deserves special attention. A small structure, built of native fieldstone to match Nassau Hall, Stanhope remains one of the most satisfying buildings on the campus. It is composed of three rectangular blocks that intersect and balance one another, projecting into space on three different axes. The resulting interplay of mass against space creates a three-dimensional quality that invites one to view the building from all sides. In Georgian architecture space was static and buildings were to be seen from the front; but in post-Colonial or Federal building, exemplified by Stanhope, space has become dynamic; one is drawn into a stimulating relationship with it. Inside, the original position of the staircase in Stanhope, on the cross axis of the building, created a complex interior core in which the spaces enclosed by the rectangular blocks of the building interpenetrated.

Although the projecting pavilion containing the main entrance is differentiated from the two other blocks by a shorter projection into space and a different orientation, it relates to them by the repetitive use of triangular pediments and round-headed windows. Within the basic arch-form of the large windows the architect has created a complicated pattern of curves and angles. To achieve further contrast in the design he has placed small rectangular windows above the dominating rounded-headed ones of the ground floor. Ornament has been suppressed in order to let the monumentality and form-space relationships speak for themselves.

Such sophisticated interrelationships of space, mass, and shape as we see in Stanhope were conceived only by professional architects or extraordinarily gifted amateurs like Thomas Jefferson. In 1804, the year Stanhope was built, Benjamin Latrobe had recently finished the reconstruction of Nassau Hall and had completed the design of "Old West" at Dickinson College, Carlisle, Pennsylvania, a building which resembles Stanhope and Nassau Hall in many respects. It is therefore reasonable to attribute to Latrobe not only the designs for Stanhope and Philosophical but also the campus plan that coordinated them.* This classic scheme for the campus was continued later with the building of East and West Colleges (1833 and 1836), and then of Whig and Clio (1837).

Unfortunately the rebuilding of Nassau Hall did not herald a rebirth of good feeling on campus. The college authorities and trustees chose to ignore the movement abroad to secularize education, while the students quite naturally embraced it. In 1807 one of the biggest riots in the history of the college erupted over the question of who was responsible for the fire five years before. The college had reached its nadir.

Many prominent Presbyterian clergymen, among them Samuel Miller and Ashbel Green, had long been alarmed about conditions at the college and anxious to establish a separate theological school. Miller had written several years before that it might be desirable "to have the divinity school uncontaminated by the college, to have its government unfettered and its orthodoxy and purity perpetual." In 1810 the Presbytery of Philadelphia introduced a widely favored proposal for a Presbyterian seminary, the first in the United States.

The Reverend Dr. Archibald Alexander was elected the first faculty member of the new institution, which met at the college from 1812 until 1817, when the first

---

* While this book was in press, examination of the heretofore inaccessible rough minutes of the college's board of trustees provided documentary confirmation of Latrobe's responsibility for the design of Stanhope and Philosophical Halls.

building (now called Alexander Hall; Fig. 68) on the new seminary campus was ready. Designed by John McComb, Jr., the well-known architect of New York's City Hall, Alexander Hall reflected the conservative, austere attitudes of the seminary trustees. As the directors' minutes say: "They have always endeavoured to combine usefulness with plainness and simplicity." Alexander Hall bears a close resemblance in material and plan to its larger neighbor, Nassau Hall, but is more pleasing in its proportions. In style, it belongs to the category of American Georgian public buildings which begins with Nassau Hall and includes Old Queen's at Rutgers, also designed by McComb. Although later in date than Old Queen's (1811), Alexander Hall is *retarda-taire* in design. Queen's, with its emphasis on contrasting spatial planes and more complex relation of shapes, is much more sophisticated and elaborate than Alexander. Only the latter's main entrance, a restoration of the original, reveals its early nine-teenth-century date in the use of an Adamesque decorative vocabulary. But in Alexander Hall McComb produced a building of good proportions, solid construction, and monumental though simple design, eminently suited for its dignified and didactic function as the seat of a Presbyterian seminary.

For several decades the seminary dominated the college, especially in disciplinary matters. The early bylaws of the college required twelve of the twenty-seven trustees to be Presbyterian ministers, and these were usually affiliated with the seminary. The successful establishment of the seminary may have thrown the strife-ridden college into eclipse, but it brought new scholars, many of them distinguished, to town; and in the long run it permitted the college to emerge from the domination of the church.

67. The Nassau Club, 6 Mercer Street. Samuel Miller came to
Princeton from New York in 1812 as one of the first two
professors of the new Theological Seminary. In July 1814
construction was begun on his residence. The site had formerly
been occupied by the home of his father-in-law, Jonathan
Dickinson Sergeant, a prominent lawyer and one of the authors
of New Jersey's Constitution; the Sergeant house had been
destroyed by fire during the British occupancy of Princeton
in December 1776. In 1903 the property was acquired by the
Nassau Club. Extensive additions were made to the rear of the
house in 1911. The Nassau Club is gracious and commodious,
but of no particular architectural distinction. It differs little
from a standard Georgian house; only the slimness of such
members as the columns, attached pilasters, and window muntins identify it as of the Federal period.

68. Alexander Hall, Princeton Theological Seminary. As architect for "Old Seminary" the Building Committee chose John McComb, Jr., who had gained distinction as designer of New York's City Hall (in collaboration with Joseph Mangin) and, closer to home, Old Queen's at Rutgers. The cornerstone was laid in September 1815 and the building was occupied for the winter session of 1818. A cupola was envisioned in the original plan, but funds were short and this embellishment was not added until 1826. (The cupola burned in 1913; its replacement was designed by W. E. Stone.) Records of the building's construction provide insight into early nineteenth-century building practices. McComb received one hundred dollars for a set of plans and five dollars a day plus expenses for the several trips he made to Princeton to observe the progress of the work. Day-to-day supervision was left to Peter Bogart, who became the seminary's first steward. Workmen's hours were from sunrise to sunset, except for Saturdays and Mondays, when the day began at 6 a.m. and ended at 6 p.m. Their remuneration ranged from $1.50 to $2.00 a day, plus "one gill & a half of ardent spirits." Whether because of or in spite of this latter provision, the work progressed with "activity, diligence and judgment."

69. The College Campus. This drawing, by an anonymous amateur, was made sometime between 1804, when work on Latrobe's reconstruction of Nassau Hall was completed, and 1833, when a long-contemplated enlargement of the Vice-President's House was carried out. Although it is probably not as accurate a representation of Nassau Hall as the lithograph made by J. H. Bufford in 1838, it is the best pictorial elucidation of the general condition of the campus in the early nineteenth century. At the left is the house originally built, in 1800, for the Professor of Mathematics, and given the name of the Vice-President's House during the long tenancies of the Mc-Leans, father and son. The trustees' specifications called for it to be built of brick, two stories high, and measuring 24 x 34 feet. There was to be an adjoining kitchen, 16 x 16 feet. The house quickly proved inadequate, and in 1823 the trustees considered enlarging it according to a plan proposed by Charles Steadman, a local builder-architect. (Steadman appeared in the role of planning architect; bids were then to be let to other contractors.) Evidently no action was taken at that time, but the house was eventually renovated in 1833-34, at which time it was enlarged to five bays and a small two-columned portico

was added. The house was demolished, along with Philosophical Hall, prior to the erection of Chancellor Green Library in 1873. To the rear of the Vice-President's House stood Philosophical Hall, built, with its mate, Stanhope Hall, on the opposite side of the campus, in 1803-04. At the same time that the trustees decided to build these two they agreed to provide a house for the Professor of Languages, shown here to the southwest of Nassau Hall. Plain in style and made of stone, it was demolished or moved when Whig and Clio Halls were begun in 1837. The trustees' minutes are silent on its fate. The house shown to the southeast of Nassau Hall, and rather far to the rear if the artist's shaky perspective is to be trusted, was probably Prospect. However crude the drawing may be, it has certainly captured the classic symmetry of the campus after the building program of 1803-04 was completed. The balance implicit in these buildings was enhanced later by the disposition of a pair of buildings, designed by the Building Committee of the Board of Trustees, East College, erected south of Philosophical Hall in 1833-34 (demolished in 1896), and West College, placed on the opposite side of the campus in 1836.

70. Archibald Alexander House. Almost as soon as Alexander Hall was completed, work was begun on a residence for the "Professor of didactick and polemick divinity," who had found his temporary rental quarters somewhat unsatisfactory. The house was occupied in 1821. Conservative in plan, the Alexander House might have been designed almost any time in the preceding fifty years. Only such details as the flat lintels and Tuscan portico betray its early nineteenth-century origin.

71. Hodge House. The house to the west of Alexander Hall was
built for Charles Hodge, who occupied it on January 1, 1825.
Originally it, like the Alexander House to the east, was of unpainted red brick. The placing of the Palladian window, with
its sunburst heading, between the first and second stories is a
sophisticated note for Princeton.

72. Greek Revival houses along Alexander Street.

VII · A RETURN TO ANTIQUITY

WHILE the college struggled, the town was booming, in part because of national prosperity, in part because of the enormous growth of stagecoaching. The inns kept as many as a hundred horses ready to supply the thirty coaches that left daily for New York and Philadelphia. Coaching days were numbered, however, for in 1832 digging began for the Delaware and Raritan Canal and by 1839 the Camden and Amboy Railroad was operating. Even before the railroad was finished a local journalist foresaw the emergence of Princeton as a commuter's haven, for he said, "The grand connecting link of CONTINUOUS Rail Road communication from Philadelphia to N. York, about to be located, will no doubt pass through a part of the Borough and add materially to the value of property in this vicinity. Citizens of N. York or Philadelphia may then have their families here, and reach their business in either place in less than THREE hours—they can now do it in less than *five*." The construction of the canal and railroad stimulated the growth of the area around the Princeton Basin, now lower Alexander Street. The old red building at the canal (Figs. 74, 75), once the Railroad Hotel, still exists as a reminder of the Basin's bustling activity more than a century ago.

The center of town grew apace. Nassau and Witherspoon Streets became inadequate to accommodate the growth. Houses sprang up in other parts of town, along Mercer and Canal (now Alexander) Streets; Steadman Street (now Library Place), Edgehill, Jackson, Green, and Quarry Streets were all laid out in the 1830's for new building. New brickyards and lumberyards found business good as building after building continued to go up. Prosperity brought paved sidewalks, public bathing rooms (which offered "warm, cold or shower baths for gentlemen"), and a tree and plant nursery. Pine Street was opened as the site of a projected silk industry. Much of the capital for this expansion was provided by the Princeton Bank, established by a group of local citizens in 1834. Growth of the cultural life of the community paralleled that of the business expansion. By the second and third decades of the nineteenth century the town had five private schools, three or four common schools, two public libraries, and professional teachers of art, voice, the dance, the flute and other musical instruments.

The increases in population led to changes in the structure of government. The impossibility of policing Nassau Street, where one could escape the jurisdiction of one county simply by stepping across the street into another, led in 1813 to the granting of a Borough Charter to Princeton. In 1838 a new county, Mercer, was formed and the outlines of Princeton Township delineated.

Such a boom in business and population with its attendant building meant that this era would stamp its physical identity on Princeton more strongly than any preceding one. On the national scene the years 1789-1820 were teeming with ferment. Politically the nation had shed its dependence on England and was embarked on a new experiment; architecturally changes of a less dramatic but significant nature were taking place. A resurgent interest in classical antique sources informed the period, derived primarily from the Adam brothers in England who in turn had been stimulated by discoveries of Roman ruins at Pompeii, Herculaneum, and especially Spalato (Yugoslavia). The Federal style, a name acquired from the contemporaneous political period, represented both the end of eighteenth-century classicism which had relied chiefly on Palladian and Renaissance sources and the beginning of a new attitude toward building which turned more and more self-consciously to past styles for the symbolism attached to them. As practiced by the few leading architects of the time, the Federal style showed new developments in spatial concepts. More complicated floor plans, using varying shapes and sizes of rooms, revealed a broadened sensitivity to functional and spatial relationships. Its regional diversity defies a simple characterization; Samuel MacIntyre's lavishly decorated Salem houses, for example, do not look like Benjamin Latrobe's simpler though still elegant Philadelphia houses. And further, the Federal style in the hands of builders in provincial centers like Princeton retained many features of Georgian architecture such as the rectangular center hall floor plan and to it applied the new decorative vocabulary: the attenuation of applied members, the delicacy of classical detail, the penchant for oval and elliptical forms, the flatness of surfaces.

During these years, 1789-1820, of searching for an architecture appropriate to its youth, vigor, and assertiveness, the new nation found its most eloquent spokesman in Thomas Jefferson. While most other builders of the late eighteenth century were using Adamesque-Federal motifs indiscriminately for their decorative value Jefferson sought inspiration directly from antique sources. He was attracted to the antique as much for its symbolic value as for its inherent aesthetic qualities. He proclaimed its moral uprightness and republican virtues in his writing and he captured its monumentality and flavor in his design for the Virginia State Capitol at Richmond (1789), a direct reference to the Roman Republican Temple, the Maison Carrée at Nîmes, France.

The revived interest in antique Roman sources, in which Jefferson was so influential, progressed logically to an investigation of Greek antiquity after about 1820. The ascendancy of Greece over Rome was preordained. Greek civilization was earlier and therefore could be considered in a sense purer. What could have been a more fitting example for the United States to follow than the birthplace of democracy? Furthermore, identification of the Roman revival with Napoleon's Empire contributed to the demise of Roman influence while the appeal of the Greek War for Independence (1821-33) was an irresistible attraction to Greece for democratic idealists in the United States.

Enthusiasm for the Greek Revival style spread throughout the country, but the actual results in building never became archaeologically exact. Greek details, often mixed with Roman, were translated into wood with freedom and ingenuity. Frequently an imaginative builder-architect invented his own vocabulary. The most famous example of this is, of course, Latrobe's corn and tobacco capitals for the United States Capitol. Never before or since in American architecture has one style so dominated the country, permeating all levels of building from the simplest domestic vernacular to the most important public official. Even more than in the eighteenth century, pattern books became the vehicle for the spread of the style. Thus the provincial carpenter could build in the same mode as his trained peers in the city. Although the self-trained builders rarely grasped the underlying principles of classical architecture, grafting their superficial details onto basically *retardataire* designs, they were able, through the pattern books and their own manual skill, to produce buildings of aesthetic, functional, and expressive value.

With the exception of the work of Latrobe and John Haviland on the college campus, to speak of early nineteenth-century architecture in Princeton is to study the work of Charles Steadman. As a businessman he flourished in this prosperous era, and, more important, as a builder-architect he marked Princeton with the indelible stamp of this national style of architecture. Steadman was born in 1790; we know nothing of his early life, but he was in Princeton in 1813 when money was subscribed to him for losses sustained in a fire. By 1820 he was employed by the First Presbyterian Church as a carpenter and had already become a solid citizen, for he was also a member of the fire company. Three years later, as assistant alderman, he made plans for a Town Hall.

By the third decade of the century Steadman was a successful and respected member of the community, partner in a lumberyard and a drygoods business. As entrepreneur, he became Princeton's first real estate developer, buying up large blocks of land, subdividing them and building houses, which he then rented or sold. In the style of modern developers, he named one of the streets he opened after himself. As a man of property, Steadman played an active role in community affairs. He was at various times a director of the Princeton Bank, a trustee of the Princeton Preparatory School, a member of the committee attempting to organize Mercer County, a member of the building committee for Trinity Church and later its first warden and a vestryman. His business activities prospered so much that in 1835-1836 when the First Presbyterian Church burned, Steadman, who had worked for the church as a carpenter for $1.50 a day ten years before, acted both as the architect and main financier for the rebuilding. Steadman's most active period as a builder was from about 1825 to 1845. After this time we know less of his work, but he was still a pillar of the church almost until the time of his death in New York in 1868.

John F. Hageman, who knew Steadman, wrote in his history of Princeton, "There was no architect and builder . . . who gave so many years and so much capital to the erection of buildings, public and private, as Charles Steadman." Steadman was a typical carpenter-builder. Beginning as a carpenter working in the traditional methods of his time, he went on to become a self-taught builder-architect, basing the designs for his buildings on a combination of his own practical knowledge and ideas he found in pattern books. His style, a mixture of both Federal and Greek Revival modes, was not great architecture; rather it was competent, practical, and pleasing to the eye in its proportions and details. The mark it has left on Princeton has done much to enhance the beauty of the town, which has never again met the consistent level of quality he maintained.

Of the more than seventy buildings attributed to Steadman, about forty are extant. One of the earliest still standing is 12 Morven Place (Fig. 83), built before 1830. It was moved to its present site in 1905 from its original position to the west of the First Presbyterian Church. 12 Morven Place is traditional in preserving the four-square plan of the Georgian house, but differs from its colonial predecessors in proportion. The ceilings are higher, while the roof is not as steeply pitched. The combined effect of these changes is to make the façade of the house seem very square and to stress the geometric volume of the cubic mass behind the façade. In decorative detail the builder has turned to classical sources, derived from the pattern books of architects such as Minard Lafever or Asher Benjamin.

His skill and freedom in handling this vocabulary is apparent in the well-carved floral motifs around the front door and the modified Roman Ionic capitals which support the roof over the single-storied portico. The windows flanking the door and directly above it are divided into three lights separated by thin pilasters and crowned with projecting lintels. These windows, together with the freestanding columns of the portico and the carved doorway, give the façade a sculptural quality in which light and shade play an important part, creating a rich contrast between mass and void. The effect is quite different from flatter, more linear eighteenth-century façades.

A more elegant and perhaps even earlier example of Steadman's work is Borough Hall (Figs. 80, 81) on Stockton Street. This house, opposite Morven, was built shortly after 1825 by Richard Stockton, the "Duke," for his daughter Annis on her marriage to Senator John Renshaw Thomson. Later alterations, notably the mansard roof, have robbed the building of some of its classic simplicity, but it still has the grand ballroom, finely detailed windows, impressive yet delicate four-columned portico, and rich black marble fireplaces, which may have been brought from New York. The handling of the details and the proportions of the building project lightness and elegance rather than heavy solemnity.

In Steadman's later buildings one notices an increasing compactness, monumentality, and more restrained use of detail. 72 Library Place (Figs. 88, 89), one of Woodrow Wilson's former residences, is a five-bay house in which the decoration is confined to the front door, the window directly above and the cornice, the latter impressively terminating and unifying the whole façade. The play of light and shadow is increased by the carving, which is more deeply incised than that of his earlier buildings.

The more characteristic, because more modest, Steadman house of the 1830's has three bays, with side entrance, in plan much like a New York or Philadelphia town house of the same period. Among the best examples are several on Alexander Street (Figs. 92-95; nos. 19, 25, 29, and 31) and Mercer Street (Fig. 96; nos. 36, 40, and 42). They may have been built on speculation and were most certainly occupied by local tradesmen. Together the group (Fig. 90) constitutes a remarkable survival of an early nineteenth-century middle class neighborhood. As such, the whole complex could serve as a model to today's developers, a visual dissertation on how to achieve variety and preserve good taste, while working within the confines of almost identical plans and lots. Though not large, these Alexander Street houses have a certain monumentality, derived from their compact cubic shape combined with solid, well-ordered classical detail and proportion. As a group they are unified by repetition of motifs, the number and spacing of the windows, and the relation of the portico to the façade. At the same time Steadman skillfully achieved variety by varying details within each house. The graceful round columns of No. 29 are juxtaposed to the square piers of its neighbor; the rectangular garret windows of No. 31 contrast with the beautiful scalloped molding of No. 29.

A tantalizing description in the *Princeton Whig* of 1836 advertised for sale at auction in New York, ". . . that elegant and Classic Grecian Doric Villa and Lot, in Princeton" and went on to describe the house, which included a bathroom with "accommodations for cold, warm, and shower baths." The inclusion of indoor bathing facilities was symptomatic of a concern for the household's convenient operation, of a trend toward the provision for solid comfort that would come to full flower in the Victorian era. If the advertisement had read "Ionic" instead of "Doric" the house in question could reasonably be identified as Drumthwacket (Figs. 116, 119), built about 1835, probably by Steadman. If indeed Steadman did build Drumthwacket, it was the most elegant of his private homes. Generally he used conservative designs for houses, restricting himself to a classical vocabulary applied to individual elements of the design—doors, windows, cornices. Drumthwacket is an exception. The entire façade is bound together by the colossal portico, embracing the full height and width of the building. The refined use of the anthemion and other classical motifs both inside and out, and the cubic monumentality of the building place it in a very different class from the simple houses of Alexander Street. Possibly the more elaborate program of Drumthwacket expressed the wishes of the architect's client, Charles Smith Olden, who had returned to his native Princeton from New Orleans in 1834 in possession of a considerable fortune. Undoubtedly in New Orleans he had admired the ample, porticoed, classic mansions then being erected by men of wealth in the Garden District and on the outlying plantations.

With the exception of Drumthwacket, Steadman reserved the more monumental and obviously classical temple types for his public buildings. Of those built in the 1830's, Princeton has two notable survivals: Miller Chapel (Fig. 122) at the seminary, erected in 1833, and the First Presbyterian Church (Fig. 123) rebuilt by Steadman in 1835-1836. In these buildings Steadman had two of his rare opportunities to produce full-blown Greek Temple types so much in vogue at the time. Miller Chapel, although small, is monumental in feeling, a quality it derives from its formal Doric portico, its severe simplicity of outline, and restrained use of decorative detail. In their use of classical details builder-architects like Steadman did not slavishly reproduce in antiquarian fashion the antique models. They used them with a freedom and often naïveté which made their work uniquely expressive of early nineteenth-century America.

The First Presbyterian Church on Nassau Street, while monumental and massive in proportion, is less severe than the Chapel. The curving Ionic capitals of the fluted columns and the egg and dart detail on the pilasters of the façade give it a more refined and regal appearance than its smaller sister. The church is especially important as a very early example of the *in antis* type of façade; that is, two free-standing columns on a recessed porch enclosed by two projecting side blocks framed by coupled *antae*, or pilasters, at the corners. This design, which had first been employed in New York four years earlier, was to become a staple of American church architecture.

Steadman also executed the original buildings of the Halls (Figs. 117, 118), Whig and Clio, based on designs by the Philadelphia architect, John Haviland. Steadman's other major designs were for the original Trinity Church and Mercer County Court House (both destroyed), the first Princeton Bank building, and probably for the First Presbyterian Church in Trenton.

Fortunately, Steadman used the temple form only where appropriate and refrained from the excesses often found in other parts of the country where Greek temples became canonic regardless of function. Perhaps the panic of 1837 helped curb an inordinate use of the temple form by slowing business activity in Princeton to a crawl. In the words of John F. Hageman, "The great financial revulsion in 1837, which spread so much desolation throughout the States, by depreciation of property and general bankruptcy, affected Princeton much, though not so much as it did many other communities." Nevertheless, in a little more than a decade, Steadman had succeeded in changing the face of Princeton. Colonial Princeton was primarily a red brick and stone village. It is Steadman's early nineteenth-century town, its placid streets lined with classically ordered white clapboard houses, that has dominated the popular image of "old Princeton."

73. Doorway, 19 Moran Avenue. The finest architectural ornament in Princeton is probably that produced in the late 1820's and 1830's. The skill of local craftsmen is evident in the classical proportions and sharply incised carving of this doorframe, preserving its dignity despite the intrusion of a Victorian door and modern siding. 19 Moran has been moved down the street from a site at the corner of Nassau Street.

74, 75. The Railroad Hotel, in the 1870's and now, lower Alexander Street and Canal Road. The present lazy and rather somnolent atmosphere gives little indication of the brisk activity that once centered on the Princeton Basin. In the early years of the nineteenth century there was enormous expansion in transportation as efforts were made to weld the new country into an economic and political entity. A network of straight turnpike roads with greatly improved surfaces was laid. Locally, the New Brunswick Straight Turnpike (Route 1) was opened in 1804. Because this diverted business from the taverns and shops of the old highway through Kingston and Princeton, a group of local businessmen procured a charter for the Princeton and Kingston Branch Turnpike (Mercer Street) in 1807. Meanwhile interest was growing in a canal to connect the Delaware and Raritan Rivers. Various attempts were made to organize a canal company and to secure a charter and adequate financing, but they all foundered until 1830, when a railroad between Camden and Perth Amboy was also being considered. A compromise was achieved between the canal interest, headed by Robert F. Stockton, and the principals of the railroad, Robert and John Cox Stevens. The canal was begun in 1830 and completed in 1834, and the railroad reached Princeton in 1839. At first the canal was to carry both freight and passengers, and in the late 1830's this Princeton building was referred to, somewhat grandly, as the Steamboat Hotel. The railroad must have been much faster, if not more comfortable, and passenger traffic on the canal was discontinued in 1835, the hotel's name eventually changing to suit the fact. At the height of its activity, Princeton Basin was a lively spot. Besides the hotel, there were two basins where barges could pull out of the traffic to load and unload; an office each for the canal, railroad, and coal companies; a railroad station; a sash and blind factory, haypress, lumberyard, and a manufacturer of iron roofing; an Episcopal Chapel; and fourteen or fifteen houses and two stores. The area gradually declined after the main tracks of the railroad were moved out to Princeton Junction in 1864. The hotel, which stands as a relic of this bustle, is an ordinary commercial building that might have been built almost any time in the nineteenth century. Based on a long vernacular tradition, these utilitarian structures are characterized by unadorned wall surfaces and simple fenestration.

76. Locomotive of the Camden and Amboy Railroad passing over the Canal Bridge in the 1860's.

77. Woodburning locomotive and car at Princeton Junction, c. 1870.

78. Mule-drawn barge on the Delaware and Raritan Canal, c. 1900.

Princeton New Jersy. September 9th 1847.
Went to See my nephew, Charles Miller.
He was A Student in the Seminary at the time.
I Stead and continue in the place one week, In the
Hotel. Kept by John De Graw. And on Sunday we
went in church hearing Rev. Dr. Alexander preach.
And at the time Saw old professor - Miller. and hearing a good
Sermon preach.

We took A walk in the Evening after my nephew had his Study.
done. And went to the Library. and to the Botanic garden
It is kept in good order, the garden is well worthy of a visit on the
13. day of September. We went to the Burying ground and Saw many
old Tomb Stones. one of old Bur - his Son has now at his grave.

79. Page from the Diary of Lewis Miller of York, Pennsylvania. No other evidence of a "Botanic garden" in Princeton exists. Perhaps Miller was depicting the "Public Garden" advertised by Peter Scudder in the *Princeton Whig* of June 24, 1836 and succeeding issues. Scudder maintained the Garden in the rear of his house on the south side of Nassau Street, a few doors east of the junction of Stockton and Mercer Streets. There, in the shelter of roofed arbors, he served pies, tarts and fruits, ice cream and beverages ". . . of the most improved and fashionable kinds." Although Miller's drawing cannot be established as an accurate depiction of any particular spot, it reflects the somnolent character of central Princeton after the canal and railroad had removed most traffic from the middle of town.

80. Thomson Hall, 50 Stockton Street. Built shortly after 1826 for John R. Thomson and his bride, Annis Stockton, on land given by her father, Richard the "Duke," Thomson Hall was one of Charles Steadman's earliest commissions. The central block is one of the finest surviving examples of late Federal architecture in Princeton. Thomson's second wife modernized the house in the 1870's with a mansard roof and other Victorian addenda.

81. Fanlight, Thomson Hall. Presented with one of his rare opportunities to design a residence for persons of wealth, Steadman proved himself less conservative than in his small houses and public buildings. Thomson Hall's symmetry and general proportions complement Morven across the road, but the sophisticated interplay of elliptical and rectangular shapes on the façade are plainly of the Federal rather than the Georgian period. Also, the rooms within are arranged asymmetrically, with more regard for function and a more complicated relation of interior spaces than Steadman usually essayed.

82. 1 Bayard Lane. Richard Stockton the "Duke" noted in his will, dated January 14, 1826, that he was leaving to his son, Robert F. Stockton, land on the north side of Nassau Street, "on which he has built, which I gave but have not yet formally conveyed to him." As his father did, when Morven required rebuilding after the fire of 1821, and like his sister Annis at Thomson Hall, Robert Stockton called on Charles Steadman to design his house. It was probably built in 1823, the year of his marriage. Later it was occupied by his brother-in-law, James Potter. A series of enlargements has been made over the years; the façade, however, has not been affected and the house is beautifully preserved. Together with Morven and Thomson Hall it constitutes a remarkable group of complementary houses built for members of one family.

83. 12 Morven Place. Built prior to 1830 on a lot directly to the west of the First Presbyterian Church, it replaced the stone tavern that occupied the site in the eighteenth century. The house was moved to its present location in 1905. Distinguished occupants have included Professors Stephen Alexander and Albert M. Dod. Steadman was already using a mixture of Roman and Greek vocabularies when he designed this façade. He had abandoned the elliptical motifs, favored in the Federal era, for rectangular forms, but the slenderness of the columns is reminiscent of the taste of a decade earlier. The wrought-iron fence in the foreground was originally erected in 1838 as the boundary between Nassau Street and the college campus fronting Nassau Hall. When FitzRandolph Gateway replaced it in 1905, the fence was moved to the grounds of the Second Presbyterian Church (St. Andrew's) at Nassau and Chambers Streets. During a restoration of the church in 1965, it was once more taken down and moved to its present site.

84. 16 Boudinot Street.

85. 44 Washington Road.

This pair of houses was built by Steadman on Washington Road in 1832. The two elderly ladies of the Olden family who commissioned them worried about undertaking so ambitious a project at their advanced age; they concluded, however, that they would be comfortable in a location so remote from the noise and bustle of town. Besides, they felt that the houses ". . . will make a very handsome appearance; they stand so high they can be seen a great ways." 16 Boudinot was moved to that location in 1930; its mate was demolished in 1962.

86. 44 Washington Road being demolished. Eighteenth- and early nineteenth-century houses were solidly built. A heavy pegged timber frame, diagonally braced, provided the main support. The interstices were filled with nogging, made, in the central New Jersey area, of crude, soft brick, which offered both further support and good insulation. A sheathing of clapboard improved the appearance of the house and helped protect the nogging from the weather. This building method was utilized by the earliest American colonists and continued in use well into the nineteenth century, when it was gradually supplanted by the balloon frame. Timber framing, which was connected by pegged or mortised and tenoned joints, was extremely sturdy; but it required skilled craftsmen, and the heaviness of the members tended to limit builders to simple rectangular forms. The balloon frame, developed in Chicago in 1833, utilized a multiplicity of thinner members, nailed to one another, and could be erected by anyone moderately apt in the use of tools. In wooden construction it made possible those variations of form and silhouette so popular in the Victorian era.

87. Beehive Oven, 44 Washington Road. The house Steadman built for Miss Olden was only one room deep, containing a wide central stair hall with parlor and dining room on the first floor and two bedrooms on each of the two floors above. It was attached to an earlier house, built in the first years of the nineteenth century, that stood at right angles to the street and evidently served as the kitchen for the new house. At the east of this southern wing was the great cooking fireplace with a beehive oven protruding to the rear. It was the last surviving exterior oven in Princeton, and, if other examples in New Jersey are any criterion, an unusually large one.

88, 89. 72 Library Place. This was one of four houses built by Steadman on the section of Library Place between Mercer and Stockton Streets. The street, which then extended no further than Stockton, was newly opened and was called Steadman Street. 72 Library Place was built in 1836 for Professor John Breckinridge of the Princeton Theological Seminary. The house, moved to this location c. 1880, was leased by Woodrow Wilson in 1890. Undoubtedly it originally had a small two-columned portico like that on the majority of Steadman's houses. This was removed and an ungainly porch added. The porch in turn was removed and the present stair added during a restoration made in the 1930's. 72 Library Place is one of the best of Steadman's houses. It shares with most of them a sense for good proportion which makes it immediately pleasing. But its chief virtue lies in the unusually fine detail, which, while restrained, is varied, and handled with a freedom and vigor that delight the eye.

89

90. West side of Alexander Street. When work was begun on the Delaware and Raritan Canal in 1832 a new road, then called Canal Street, was opened from Mercer Street to the Basin. Wooden sidewalks were laid to counteract the Princeton mud and new buildings for both residential and business use were erected. Charles Steadman, as astute as a businessman as he was skilled as a builder, grasped the opportunity offered by the opening of this new artery. His own lumberyard and carpenter's shop were located on Canal Street, convenient to the new canal and the railroad which soon followed it. In addition he purchased large parcels of property along the street and along Mercer Street at its head. Through the 1830's and 40's he subdivided his holdings, building a series of relatively small but handsome houses, which he sold or rented. Occasionally he seems to have utilized remnants of earlier farm buildings in these houses. Despite this incorporation and the relatively long time-span covered in their erection, the Alexander Street houses achieve a considerable sense of unity. The close-ranked façades are a theme with variations, in which the rhythm of related cornices and twin-columned porticos is enlivened by the diversity of decorative detail. The northern end of Alexander Street is Princeton's first, and probably best, example of cohesive urban design, comparable in kind, if not in quality, to the carefully planned Greek Revival rows of New York and Philadelphia

91. East side of Alexander Street.

92

93

92-95. Houses along the west side of Alexander Street.

94

95

96. 36 and 40 Mercer Street. The former was built for James S. Green, son of Ashbel Green. The imposing double house at the corner was built prior to 1839, when it and the adjoining house on Alexander Street were sold for $3700, a handsome sum for that day.

96

97

98

97-100. Houses along the east side of Alexander Street.

99

100

101. South side of Mercer Street, west of the Edgehill Street intersection.

101

102

102, 104. 29 Alexander Street. In its original modest plan this was typical of the Alexander Street houses. On the ground floor a side hall opened onto double parlors. The second floor contained two bedrooms above the parlors plus a minuscule hall bedroom. The garret contained two more bedrooms. Kitchen and service areas were at the rear. Most of these houses have been considerably enlarged at the back. The detail of 29 is particularly interesting. In the cornice a row of dentils is played against a scalloped row of drops. Freely imagined columns of Corinthian derivation support the portico.

103. Doorway, 20 Alexander Street. There appears to be some discrepancy between the semi-circular fanlight, a motif which fell into disuse after the early 1830's, and the simplified block forms of the square columns and bracketed entablature, which reflect the Tuscan Revival of the mid-1840's. Perhaps Steadman, during his later work on Alexander Street, modernized the doorway, adding the portico to bring this house into conformity with its neighbors.

104

105. 108 Mercer Street. Built on Alexander Street by Steadman for William Neal in 1833, this house was moved to its present location in 1876. It originally stood in front of Stuart Hall. A house of almost identical design is at 25 Vandeventer Avenue.

106. Einstein House, 112 Mercer Street. At the same time another Alexander Street house, this one built by Samuel Stevens, was moved to the lot adjacent to the Neal house. Albert Einstein, who arrived in Princeton in 1933, occupied this dwelling from 1935 until his death.

107. The Manse, 26 Library Place. During its first forty years the Presbyterian Church made no special provision for housing its ministers. In 1804 Dr. Thomas Wiggins, physician, former treasurer of the college, and trustee of the church, died, leaving his brick house and twenty acres of land to the Church. The house, now destroyed, stood on Wiggins Street on the site now occupied by a power station. Probably built in the third quarter of the eighteenth century, it was similar in type to Constitution Hill (Fig. 23). It was used as a parsonage until 1847, when house and property were sold, part of the land being incorporated into the cemetery. Once again the pastor was without an official residence. In 1860 the congregation agreed to purchase the property of Jacob W. Lane, on what was then Steadman Street. As constructed in the mid-1830's this was a three-bay house, the southern end being the older portion. The two bays to the north were probably added at the time of the church's purchase, but in a style wholly consonant with the original. 26 Library Place remained the manse of the First Presbyterian Church for a hundred years. It is now privately owned.

108. 86 Stockton Street. Like 26 Library Place this was originally a three-bay house. The eastern section was not added until the late 1920's. It can be dated in the mid-1830's, as it closely resembles the group of houses built then on Library Place. The colossal pilasters at the corners, a Greek Revival motif common elsewhere but rare in Princeton, appear also in Steadman's building for the Princeton Banking Company (Fig. 126). This was probably one of the houses that Steadman built and maintained as a rental property. He sold it in 1867 to Sarah S. Baker. He was then apparently liquidating his Princeton properties preparatory to moving to New York City, where he died in 1868. An advertisement for the sale of a neighboring property in 1836 suggests that "It is in a respectable neighborhood and in a desirable part of town."

109. 92 Stockton Street. Said to be Steadman's last construction, this house was completed just before the outbreak of the Civil War. The somewhat cramped proportions of the façade and the relative crudity of the ornament indicate that Steadman was far less comfortable in the Victorian idiom than he had been in the Greek Revival style. The adjacent property to the west was the site of the Edgehill School, a boys' preparatory school founded in 1829. Its main buildings, designed by Steadman, burned in 1925.

110, 111. Joseph Henry House. Even for a town in which some sixty buildings have been transferred from their original locations to new sites, the peripatetic Joseph Henry House on the university grounds must hold some sort of record. Erected in 1837 between West College and Stanhope Hall, it was first moved across the campus in 1870 to make way for Reunion Hall. In 1925, when the present chapel was under construction, the house was transplanted to the southwest corner of Washington Road, only to be moved once again when the site was needed for the Firestone Library. It now stands northeast of Nassau Hall. It was probably designed by Henry himself, who, in addition to his distinguished career as a physicist, taught an elective course in architecture. At the same time that the board of trustees agreed to provide Henry with a new house, they approved a plan he had presented for the future disposition of buildings on the campus. In particular, Henry's plan was followed for the placing of Whig and Clio Halls, flanking Nassau Hall at the rear. Henry's house was similar in proportion to the five-bay houses built by Charles Steadman. The present exterior ornament is largely the product of modern restoration, but even the original (as shown in the old photograph) lacked the refinement of which Steadman was capable.

112. 34 Edgehill Street. So pervasive was the Greek Revival in Princeton, that W. E. Stone's reuse of its forms in this 1902 house blended easily into the streetscape. Stone, however, like many academic revivalists, probably turned to books, rather than the local scene, for his prototype. He designed, therefore, a house with gable end to the street, a Greek Revival form popular elsewhere in the United States but rare in Princeton. He also freely intermixed forms from other periods, such as the round-headed window in the pediment and the hooded doorway.

113. Sheldon House, 10 Mercer Street. The full Greek Revival temple form, uncommon in houses in Princeton, was extremely popular both in the South and in New England. This example was moved, by canal barge, from Northampton, Massachusetts, in 1868.

114. Doorway, 36 Mercer Street.

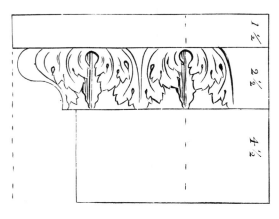

115. Plate from William Pain, *The Practical Carpenter or Youth's Instructor*, 1794. The average builder-architect of the eighteenth and early nineteenth century depended heavily on pattern books. Without formal training, he could turn to the pattern books, not only for suggestions on detail but for the simple mathematics needed to arrive at the proportions of a façade or the pitch and support of a roof. Steadman undoubtedly used pattern books extensively, although he did not follow them slavishly. Individual motifs may be reminiscent of the sketches of Pain, Asher Benjamin, John Haviland, or Minard Lafever, but Steadman used Greek forms freely, marking his buildings with the stamp of his own taste and craftsmanship.

116. Doorway, Drumthwacket, 344 Stockton Street. Charles Smith Olden served as New Jersey's Governor during the Civil War. He had made a comfortable fortune in New Orleans, returned to his native Princeton in 1834, and proceeded to com-mission the town's most grandiose Greek Revival mansion. Only the center block of Drumthwacket (Fig. 119) was built for Olden. In 1896 the property was acquired by Moses Taylor Pyne, who enlarged the house to its present dimensions.

117, 118. Whig and Clio Halls. If houses with full Greek temple fronts were rare in Princeton, public buildings were not. In 1835 a building committee of the Cliosophic Society met to consider a new building. They chose John Haviland of Philadelphia as their architect and Steadman as their builder. Not to be outdone, the American Whig Society commissioned Steadman to erect ". . . an edifice agreeable in its outline and general features to a design furnished by Mr. Haviland to the Committee of the Cliosophic Society . . . the edifice to be of stone . . . rough cast in the best manner. . . ." The resulting twin buildings were modeled on a specific prototype, the temple at Teos; the capitals copied the temple on the Ilissus. Work on both was begun in 1837 and completed in 1838. They were demolished in 1893 when the present Halls were erected.

119. Drumthwacket in the 1870's.

120. Clio Hall. The strong monumentality of Haviland's forms must have been particularly congenial to Steadman, who showed a preference for equally powerful forms in his own designs for public buildings.

121. The Cloaca Maxima. Even sanitary facilities shared the vogue for the classic. Discreetly designated in Latin, this trabeated communal convenience was built in 1837, behind and between Whig and Clio Halls.

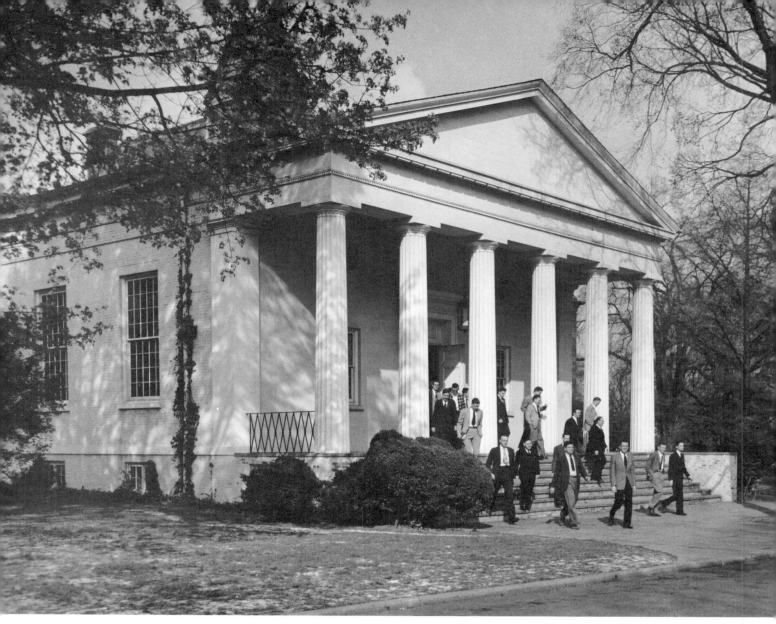

122. Miller Chapel, Princeton Theological Seminary. Built by Charles Steadman in 1833 on a site directly to the east and to the rear of Alexander Hall, Miller Chapel originally faced Mercer Street. A twin edifice to the west of Alexander Hall was projected but never built. Had it been, the effect would have been remarkably similar to that achieved five years later at the college with the placement of Whig and Clio. Miller Chapel's simple but majestic Doric façade harmonized well with the existing buildings on the seminary campus. In 1874 the chapel was "victorianized," with stained glass windows, carpeting, and upholstered pews. In 1933 a restoration was undertaken by the firm of Delano and Aldrich. The chapel was moved to its present site and enlarged by the addition of an extra bay at the rear. Most of the interior, including the chancel, dates from this restoration, but the carving of the gallery parapet and the columns supporting it are original.

123. The First Presbyterian Church. There has been a Presbyterian church on this site since work was begun on the first building in 1762. Completed in 1766, this was a simple brick meetinghouse, domestic in scale, with a gabled roof. The long side, facing Nassau Street, was pierced by two doors. Within, pews occupied the center and all four walls, except for a pulpit in the middle of the south wall. Winding staircases in the north corners led to galleries surrounding all but the south wall. The church was occupied by soldiers of both sides during the Revolution and much damaged. It burned in 1813 and a new edifice, completed the following year, was erected on the foundations of the old church, but with two entry doors on the west end and a semicircular apse at the east. Its chief decorative feature was pointed Gothic windows, a remarkably early instance of their use. In 1835 this church, too, burned. The erection of the new building was entrusted to Charles Steadman, the work being completed in 1838. The dimensions were then 60 x 80 feet. In 1874 the church was enlarged to the south, fitted with stained glass windows and redecorated under the direction of J. S. D'Orsay of New York. In 1922 the church was once again renovated. Fortunately, the sanctuary, with the exception of the south end, has retained much of Steadman's original woodwork.

124. Detail, Fence, Trinity Churchyard. Wrought-iron and later cast-iron fences were very popular from the second quarter of the nineteenth century. They, too, often reflected the interest in Greek forms.

125. Trinity Church. In 1827 a committee met to raise funds for the erection of an Episcopal church. Construction began in 1833. The edifice, completed in 1834, was of roughcast stone, with a prostyle portico of six wooden columns. The church was raised on a high podium, allowing ample room in the basement for a Sunday School. The interior was painted white. Stairs within the vestibule led to the organ loft and galleries. Although Bishop Doane, who consecrated the church, wrote that it was "admired by all for its architectural beauty," the building was destroyed in 1868 to make way for the present edifice. It survives only in this one photograph, somewhat overwhelmed by the Parish School built in 1849.

126. 4 Nassau Street. The building (far right) was erected in 1836 to house the Princeton Banking Company, forerunner of the Princeton Bank and Trust, and its head cashier. In its original state it was a not altogether successful combination of Steadman's public and domestic styles. The temple form, associated by Steadman with public buildings, is suggested in the pediment crowning the central bay and in the colossal pilasters marking the corners. Venetian three-light windows, like those used in several of his houses, adorn the central bay of the upper floor and the two side bays of the lower. The portico is a compromise; reaching neither the full height nor width of the building, it is still larger and more massive than that of any Steadman domestic building. 4 Nassau was purchased in 1896 by W. C. C. Zapf, who made extensive alterations, destroying whatever harmony the façade once possessed. The building to the left is the Corner Store, built in 1845 and long a Princeton landmark.

125

126

127. Trinity Parish School. By 1849, fifteen years after the Doric Trinity Church was consecrated, Princeton's interest in Greek forms had been largely exhausted, although a Greek style Methodist church was dedicated in 1849 and a Baptist church on Alexander Street in 1851. The new building was Gothic, evoking, in a romantic rather than archaeological vein, images of an English country church.

VIII · ROMANTICISM AND REVIVALS

AFTER the panic of 1837, the general expansion of the town proceeded at a much abated rate. Building activity did not resume until the 1840's, and most of the buildings erected during this period fall into two categories: churches, and the series of mansions for the Stocktons and their relatives. Before the boom of the 1830's Princeton was composed, religiously and ethnically, mainly of a few Quakers, a few French Huguenots, and many Presbyterians, all of English, Scotch, or Scotch-Irish background. But the boom brought new groups who in the following decades founded their own churches: Episcopalian, Roman Catholic, Methodist, and Baptist. The Stocktons, who had suffered comparatively little from the panic of 1837 because of the continued success of the canal and railroad, commissioned several grandiose dwellings. Thomas Potter, brother-in-law of Commodore Robert Stockton, turned the Prospect property into a showplace, adorned by the latest in Tuscan villas. Richard Stockton Field built Fieldwood (now Guernsey Hall), and the Commodore himself established his children in Westland (on Hodge Road), Springdale (seminary campus), and Walter Lowrie House (Stockton Street).

When these buildings were constructed, in the 1840's and 1850's, the Classical Revival had been superseded by new styles from the past. The Classical Revival, after all, had been only the first manifestation of a consciousness of the history of architecture. The new interest in history also manifested itself in fields other than architecture. In the 1840's the New Jersey Historical Society held some of its earliest meetings in Princeton and newspaper editorials urged the readers to collect documents relating to the State's colonial era. In architecture interest turned to the Middle Ages and the Renaissance as well as antiquity. These styles were revived according to their specific moral, political, or religious symbolism. Thus the Gothic carried Christian connotations; Egyptian signified permanence; and Classical, democracy. Architects came to employ different styles for different purposes. Each architect was capable of designing in a variety of modes.

Along with the interest in history and historic styles of the past, the nineteenth century had a romantic yearning for the remote in time and exotic in place. This was particularly true of the Early Victorian period. Architectural historians have, with good reason, divided the nineteenth century into three parts: Early Victorian, extending roughly from 1830 to 1860, High Victorian from 1860 to 1885, and Late Victorian from 1885 to 1920. The first phase was characterized by a revival of several past architectural styles, each kept separate from the others, but all revived simultaneously. High Victorian, which followed the Civil War, customarily combined various elements from different styles into a single building in an effort to be original. This resulted in a picturesque eclecticism which gave us much highly creative and original architecture as well as much bad. Late Victorian, extending into the twentieth century, contained a dominant element of academic revivalism and a minor but ultimately victorious element of progressivism, in which were contained the seeds of modern architecture.

By the third and fourth decades of the nineteenth century the United States, recovered somewhat from the prejudices engendered by the Revolution, was willing to turn once again to England for cultural inspiration. Since the late eighteenth century the Gothic Revival and the cult of the picturesque had dominated English architecture. Greatly influenced by Horace Walpole and his Gothic showplace, Strawberry Hill, other Englishmen built Gothic houses, often fantastic and extravagant, surrounding them with a natural, albeit contrived, setting of winding paths, woods, gazebos, artificial ruins, and the like.

The great American interpreter and popularizer of this style was Andrew Jackson Downing. Downing not only practiced landscape architecture himself, but wrote books illustrating designs for Gothic country houses which displaced the old builder's guides and became indispensable pattern books for the builders of the day. In calling for honesty, beauty, and truth in architecture and supplying designs which he claimed fulfilled these requirements, Downing created a new mode of domestic building in America which combined utility and picturesqueness. His designs offered functional floor plans adapted to suburban living and picturesque irregularity of elevation which appealed to mid-century romanticism. By means of projecting bays, balconies and windows the interior space of a house was related to the space outside. Verandas were introduced, making a transition from inside to outside and enabling the house to embrace, as it were, the nature around it. The new architecture put man in a position to communicate with nature and to identify himself with it. Reversing the trend of the Classical Revival, Downing insisted on the adaptation of the house to its site, the imitation in its silhouette of the irregular outlines of nature, and the blending of the colors with the surroundings.

Although there was some reflection of Downing's ideas on architecture in Princeton in the 1840's and 1850's there is no building directly derived from his pattern books. Perhaps the closest Princeton came to reproducing a Downing design was the original frame building of the Second Presbyterian Church (Fig. 130), now buried in a commercial structure at 190 Nassau Street (Fig. 131). The building's design incorporated both Downing's favored vocabulary—rustic Gothic—and his preferred mode of construction—vertical board and batten siding. The Early Victorian concern for nature applied not only to landscape and the relation of a building to its site, but to the selection and use of materials. Wood was used to emphasize rather than disguise its inherent characteristics and to reveal rather than conceal the structure of the building. It was in landscape design that Princeton most directly felt the influence of A. J. Downing. His plea for "smiling lawns" to accompany his "tasteful cottages" found sympathetic response. In the Princeton *Whig* of 1845 Alpha wrote, "And however small a residence may be, if it be kept well painted, well repaired, and well surrounded with trees and shrubbery, it will wear an appearance of comfort and neatness, and will speak favorably for the character of the occupant."

An intimate colleague of Downing, who contributed designs to his pattern books, John Notman, worked for the Stocktons of Princeton both as architect and as landscape designer. For Notman, as for Downing, the design of the setting was as important as the design of the house. Notman's plans for the grounds of Guernsey Hall (Fig. 142), the laying out of which occupied several years before the house was built in the late 1840's, have been preserved in a water-color drawing in the collection of the Princeton University Library. Evident in the drawing are the architect's concern for the site and orientation of the house and also his meticulous attention to drives, walks, groves and trees, outbuildings, and lawns. All considerations were subordinated to emphasizing the natural terrain and stressing the gently rolling quality of the land. Today the grounds of Guernsey Hall, now Marquand Park, are still noted for their beautiful plantings and unusual specimens.

Guernsey Hall (Fig. 138) is only one example of the suburban villa type which Notman, under the influence of Downing, had built for patrons all over the Delaware Valley. To Downing, with his eloquent description of a semi-rural but highly civilized domestic life, must go the credit for the major impetus toward the development of the suburb in America. Notman, a Scottish-born mason who had emigrated to Philadelphia about 1831, soon became a fashionable architect there. The Stockton family of Princeton, with its close ties to Philadelphia, quite naturally commissioned Notman to design three of the five large homes they built in this period. Prospect (Figs. 140, 141), Walter Lowrie House (Fig. 139), and Guernsey Hall are all exercises in the Tuscan or Italianate mode, a style more suited to expensive tastes than the Gothic cottage type, and one that combined some of the classical elements associated with city architecture with picturesque qualities more appropriate to the country. Guernsey Hall with its irregular arrangement of rectangular shapes, balustraded balconies, sharply projecting cornice, and flat-roofed tower with arched windows is typical of the group. The simplicity of its basic shapes is disguised by its irregular silhouette and the elaborate coloristic effects of the stonework and cast iron.

In 1855 when the inflammable Nassau Hall (Fig. 137) burned again, Notman was chosen to restore it. His work, while adding yet another chapter to the building's already great burden of history, did not improve it architecturally. In accord with contemporary taste, Notman replaced the pediments of the central pavilion with heavy Tuscan arches, enlarged the cupola, and added four-story square towers to either end of the building. With the exception of the towers, which were subsequently truncated, this revision of Notman's is essentially the Nassau Hall of today.

Even before the disruption caused by the Civil War, expansion of population and building in Princeton had declined. The town did not enjoy the rapid industrial and

131

economic expansion experienced by many American towns both before and after the war. There were many in Princeton who were perfectly satisfied with this situation but there were others, we learn from contemporary newspapers, who were not. In 1855 a letter in the *Princeton Press* complained about the lethargy that had kept the town from growing in the past decade, attributing it to the college which had left "no stone unturned to retard the growth of the town," and to the rich men who had bought up the land, refusing to sell and investing their capital elsewhere. The houses that were built in the 1850's and 1860's conformed to the main trend of the time, the stick style, a type of wooden architecture which grew directly out of Downing's ideas and emphasized the skeletal framework of the house.

In the decades immediately following the Civil War, large-scale building activity in Princeton centered chiefly on the campus. Commodore Stockton, who had brought his family fortunes to their apogee through investment in the canal and railroad, left them, at his death in 1866, at their lowest ebb. No other family replaced the Stocktons as patrons of architecture, but the college entered on a period of great physical expansion and academic innovation.

At the beginning of the war, almost half the student body had withdrawn to return South; at its close, the composition of the student body changed slowly from sons of the plantation aristocracy to pious Presbyterians and the scions of the industrial families of the north and east. This made new sources of wealth available to the college, which under the able leadership of President James McCosh (1868-88) devoted them to the construction of at least ten buildings. By McCosh's time architectural style had entered a new stage, had changed from Early Victorian associational revivals to a more complicated and less specific evocation of the past in general. The comparatively restrained Gothic of Downing and the subdued elegance of Notman's Tuscan gave way to a flamboyant, ostentatious architecture in which picturesque massing of forms and freedom of design are two of the most distinctive marks. Combining elements from many past styles, these High Victorian architects achieved an architecture based on freedom of interpretation and delight in the extravagant use of detail. How suitable it was to a society amassing wealth at unheard-of speed unhampered by any governmental restrictions! This was the era of crockets, finials, brackets, mansard roofs, and dripping bargeboards. "Mansard madness," derived from the French Renaissance via Napoleon III and the Second Empire, infected the whole country. While Princeton had no large outbreak of this epidemic, it had its share of the mansard style. In town, Dickinson Street and University Place were dotted with mansard roofs. On the campus, Reunion Hall (1870; demolished 1964) represented one of the few excursions of the college into this style.

Of the buildings which mushroomed in the northeast corner of the campus during McCosh's reign only one remains, the Chancellor Green Library (Figs. 152, 153;

now the Student Center). Designed by the New York architect William Appleton Potter and erected in 1873, it is a triumph of the Venetian Gothic Revival which John Ruskin so articulately championed and which is therefore often called Ruskinian Gothic. In contrast to the combination of rectangular blocks characterizing the Tuscan, this Venetian style uses variations of rounded shapes to form its composition. In Chancellor Green the octagonal central pavilion is joined by short passageways to flanking wings which are elongated octagons. Each side of the central octagon is crowned by a pediment pierced by cinquefoil arched windows. These pediments are in turn surmounted by finials leading to a central octagonal lantern, itself terminated by an intricate metal ornament. The skilled handling of masses, the subtle interplay of different shapes, and the coloristic effects achieved through the use of reddish-brown rusticated stone and varicolored roof tiles make the building a delight to the eye.

At the same time that President McCosh was overseeing the major building program at the college, the seminary was also adding to its campus, although on a smaller scale. As a result of the building activity at both institutions, many workers came to Princeton in the later seventies, built houses for themselves, and enriched the local tradesmen. The town thus emerged briefly from its lethargy of the previous decades. This short-lived activity depended solely on the activities of the college and the seminary. By the mid-eighties, we learn from the *Princeton Press*, conditions in town had returned to a low ebb and trade was dull.

The direction architecture took in the United States in the late 1870's and early eighties was profoundly influenced by the Philadelphia Centennial of 1876, which focused attention especially on English Tudor and Japanese architecture. The imaginative uses of wood in the Centennial buildings gave a fresh impetus to the continuing tradition of wooden domestic architecture in this country. These English and Japanese influences combined with the established stick style in America to form a simplified style of building known as the Queen Anne, which flourished for about fifteen years, until almost 1890. Princeton's share of Queen Anne may be seen on such streets as Dickinson, Wiggins, and University Place. Contemporaneously, of course, people continued to build in the stick and mansard styles as well.

Concurrently with the Queen Anne vogue in domestic building went a generalized and widespread Romanesque Revival in public and institutional building. The Romanesque Revival was by no means strictly archaeological, but it did stress the stony solidity and simple round arch of medieval Romanesque architecture. Compared to the extravagant High Victorian Picturesque Eclecticism of the sixties and seventies, this Romanesque Revival, like the Queen Anne, marked a return to simpler shapes and an emphasis on the solidity of the wall and on the structure of the building itself. On both the college and seminary campuses the Romanesque Revival was represented by buildings of two New York architects, Richard Morris Hunt and William Appleton Potter.

Hunt, like others of his generation, was trained in Paris and was one of the architects who introduced the Romanesque idiom to the United States. Although most famous for his French Renaissance designs executed for the Vanderbilts and others, his most distinguished building in Princeton, Marquand Chapel (Fig. 156), destroyed by fire in 1920, was in the Romanesque idiom. In the words of Montgomery Schuyler, the outstanding critic of Victorian architecture, Marquand Chapel was "individual and unconventional."

William A. Potter's work in Princeton spanned the last three decades of the nineteenth century. After a period concerned chiefly with Ruskinian interpretations of the Gothic Revival, he fell under the influence of Henry Hobson Richardson's version of Romanesque. Richardson, the best and justifiably most famous architect of his time, used a modified version of Romanesque as the vehicle for expressing his understanding of structure and his concern for the massiveness of the wall and simplification of shapes and plan. In Alexander Hall (Figs. 158-160; university campus) Potter revealed that he understood the lesson of the master. He successfully solved the problem of designing a college assembly hall, providing a large area of free-flowing space in the ambulatory which embraces three-quarters of the building. Through the consistent use of strong basic shapes and the rich but refined use of ornament and textural contrasts, he gave scale and monumentality to the building.

Although building activity in the years 1840-1890 remade the face of the college and seminary campuses, it had much less effect on the character of the town, which continued to retain the stamp of the Classical Revival. It was the new concepts of landscape design derived from Downing that left the most permanent mark of this period on the town. They were evident in the emergence of civic pride in the appearance of individual properties, in the professional landscape designing for local estates like Guernsey Hall and Lowrie House, and in the landscape planning of the college campus. Princeton is still renowned for its beautiful gardens and trees.

During the first half of the twentieth century it was fashionable to ridicule the extravagances of Victorian building, but historical perspective has made us realize the many positive contributions it made to architecture. There appeared a new freedom and functionalism in design, a sensitiveness to the characteristics of materials and an ingenuity in their use, an emphasis on structural elements, and a new sense of space which expressed itself in the more flexible free-flowing plans. An effort to bring interior and exterior space in close communication and a concern for orientation to site and surroundings consistently informed early and High Victorian architecture. Exuberance and vitality gave an originality of design and sense of scale we cannot help but admire, even envy.

128. Project for renovating 134-136 Nassau Street. Princeton has always been a conservative town, with all the attendant consequences, both good and bad. Slow to accept new methods and new styles, this conservatism has sometimes resulted in the production of architecture unresponsive to the practical and aesthetic needs of a growing community. On the other hand, Princeton's resistance to change has been responsible for the preservation of a large number of structures. The incidence of buildings which, having outlived their usefulness at one site, have been moved to another is unusual. So too, a number of buildings have been renovated one or more times. These alterations have not always been successful, but they have at least had the effect of retarding the process of destruction and allowing new generations to contemplate the merits or defects of landmarks of the past. The projected alteration of 134-136 Nassau Street, by M. H. Scott, an architect whose work is otherwise unknown, is a particularly interesting one, although it was never carried out and the building was ultimately demolished in 1881. Behind the façade proposed by Scott lies a sober straightforward house of the type built in Princeton from the Georgian era through the Greek Revival. From the appearance of its windows it might have been built around 1830. Scott proposed to overlay this with a false front drawn from a fanciful Gothic repertoire, including Tudor arches, diamond-paned casements, columns with cusped arches, and a battlement. The concept of this ornament as a thin skin applied quite superficially, its blockiness, and its consistency (it is all derived, albeit romantically and not precisely, from English Gothic and Tudor sources) bear the hallmarks of the Early Victorian period. The design was probably drawn in the late 1840's or early 1850's.

129. Springdale, 86 Mercer Street. Now the official residence of the president of Princeton Theological Seminary, Springdale was built in the late 1840's for Richard, eldest son of Commodore Robert F. Stockton. In contrast to the classically symmetrical houses built earlier for members of the Stockton family, Springdale was romantically picturesque with its vertical, irregular silhouette and its variety of ornament. But a hundred years of classical heritage were not so readily overthrown. Each separate mass of the building was still clearly defined, without the blending and indefiniteness of outline that was to characterize later Victorian architecture.

130, 131. Old Second Presbyterian Church, 190-192 Nassau Street, then and now. In December 1848 the *Princeton Whig* reported that "The Building Committee of the Second Presbyterian Church have contracted for a church edifice 70 by 32 feet with tower, somewhat after the old English style of building—steep roof, pointed windows, diamond sash, etc. The plan was drawn by Mr. Notman, the architect . . . of the Law School. . . ." The building was afterwards turned on the lot and converted to a double house. It is now an office building.

132. Lenox Reference Library, Princeton Theological Seminary. Built in 1842 and demolished in 1955, this was the finest of Princeton's Early Victorian Gothic buildings. While the unknown architect clung to a simple rectangular plan, he was no longer concerned with delimiting fixed areas of space. Large windows dissolved the heavy walls, so that indoors and outdoors seemed to become one. Aspiring pinnacles pierced the sky. Building and nature were no longer seen as separate, but as inextricably linked, just as the Gothic style was meant to link the building with the religious and educational systems of the past.

133. St. Andrew's Church (formerly the Second Presbyterian Church), Nassau and Chambers Streets. By 1868 both the First Church and the old Second Church were full. A new church was therefore planned and the building contract given to Henry W. Leard. Hageman cited Leard as ". . . the most prominent builder next to Mr. Steadman. . . ." Whether he designed the church is uncertain. No body of his work in Princeton has ever been identified for comparison, although he was evidently responsible for the beautiful "Carpenter's Gothic" Dutch Reformed Church in Rocky Hill.

134. Trinity Church, 33 Mercer Street. Although other styles had superseded the Gothic for other purposes, it was still considered the most appropriate style for churches when the present Trinity Church was built in 1868. This photograph includes the additions made when the building was renovated in 1914-1915 by Ralph Adams Cram.

135. Trinity Church. This old photograph shows the original appearance of the design of R. M. Upjohn, son of the architect of New York's Trinity Church.

136. Old St. Paul's Church. This was the third edifice built for Princeton's Roman Catholic community. Erected in 1869, it was much changed by the addition of a new front in 1912 and torn down prior to the erection of the present building in 1954.

137. Nassau Hall. This lithograph, published in 1860 by what the *Princeton Press* called "our enterprising fellow townsmen, McGinness & Smith," shows Nassau Hall as it looked after John Notman finished his Italianate rebuilding, following the disastrous fire of 1855.

138. Guernsey Hall, 63 Lovers Lane. As Charles Steadman had epitomized Princeton building during the 1830's, so John Notman epitomized the architecture of the 1840's and 1850's. Capable, like most Early Victorian architects, of designing in a number of styles, he chose the Tuscan or Italianate Revival both for Nassau Hall and for the series of villas he designed for the Stockton family. Guernsey Hall, originally called Fieldwood, was built c. 1850 for Richard Stockton Field. From 1887 to 1951 it belonged to Professor Allan Marquand and his family, who gave the house its present name. In 1912 the house was considerably altered and enlarged by the architectural firm of Cross and Cross. The wrought-iron pillars in the form of grapevines, visible in this old photograph, were removed at that time.

139. Walter Lowrie House, 83 Stockton Street. This house was built for John Potter Stockton. His young wife, Sarah Marks Stockton, kept a delightful and detailed diary, which (among notes of her frequent indispositions, gossip, and accounts of social events and shopping sprees) contains a full account of the building of her new home. Planning began in January 1848. On February 1 and 2 Notman visited the young Stocktons, showed them sketches and discussed ideas. On February 3 they visited his McCall House in Trenton. By the end of the month Notman's final plans were presented; work was begun that spring. It proceeded apace, although young Mrs. Stockton, who was living with her in-laws, found it hard to wait for completion. The exterior was largely completed by August; and Notman, with the deep concern for an appropriate setting common to the era, brought his plans for landscaping the grounds. In October the Stocktons went to Philadelphia to choose furnishings, garnet velvet and rosewood for one parlor and green and rose for the other. They moved in in June of 1849 and Mrs. Stockton wondered "how I shall behave under my new honours as mistress of the finest house in P— and one of the finest in N.J." She did not have to bear her honors long. In 1858 her

husband became Minister to the Papal States and in 1860 the house was sold to Paul Tulane. It has recently been given to Princeton University as a guest house, named for its last owner. Later owners have made various changes, but it is still clear that like the majority of Notman's Princeton buildings this was in the Italianate mode. Indeed Notman had a long-standing predilection for the style, for he had designed what was possibly the first Italianate villa in America, Bishop George Washington Doane's "Riverside" at Burlington in 1837. By 1850 the Tuscan Revival had almost superseded the Gothic in popularity, although styles were usually selected because they bore associations appropriate to a building's function. Thus Gothic remained in favor for schools, churches, and country cottages, while civic buildings were still often clothed in forms of classical derivation. The Italianate style, combining elements of the classic in its rectangular masses and simple rectangular or round-arched openings with some of the picturesque irregularity in composition and ornament, was considered particularly suitable for the suburban villa with its mingling of country and urban surroundings.

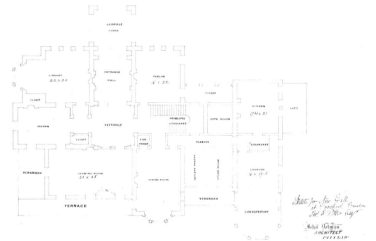

140. Proposed elevation and floor plan of Prospect.

Prospect, the official residence of Princeton University's presidents since 1879, was built by Notman for Thomas F. Potter in 1852. In preparing the site both the eighteenth-century Prospect and the old Academy on Washington Road were demolished. The plans for the house are particularly interesting. They show clearly that the irregularities of silhouette common in the Victorian era satisfied not only aesthetic requirements, but functional ones. No longer were room sizes and circulation limited by arbitrary dictates of symmetrical form, as they had been in the Georgian period. Now the most important rooms took precedence, and interior space flowed freely from room to room to provide easy access in public areas, or was carefully controlled to allow privacy where needed. The changes from the suggested elevation to the finished house are also striking. The castellated tower with its minaret and the two gables of the proposal have given way to a thoroughly integrated grouping of boxy masses with similar rooflines, thereby greatly strengthening the composition.

141. Prospect in the late 1870's.

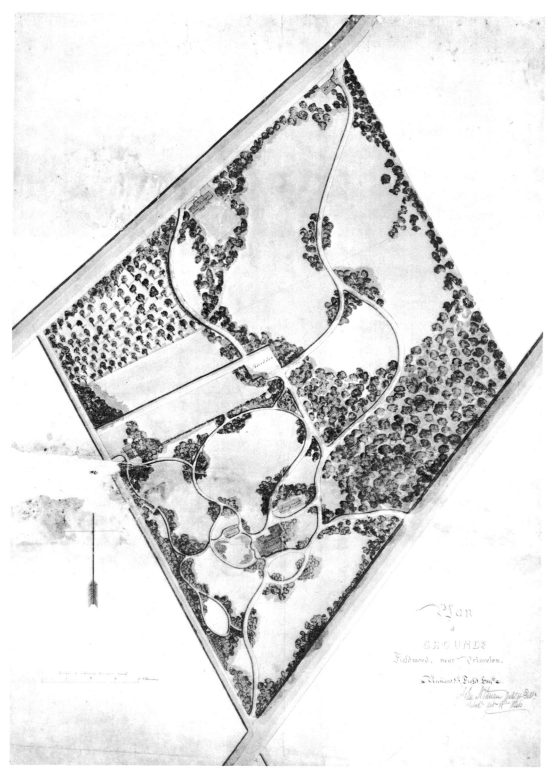

142. Landscape proposal for Fieldwood (Guernsey Hall). To Notman the surroundings of a building were evidently of almost as much importance as the building itself. Although the house at Fieldwood was not built until the early 1850's, this plan was drawn in 1846 and the intervening years spent in the acquisition of choice horticultural specimens. The Victorian planner was no longer interested in surmounting nature and forcing it into formal patterns as had been done in Morven's gardens. Rather he recognized nature's wildness and rejoiced in it. His desire was to accentuate those aspects of nature which were most picturesque, enhancing them with winding drives and carefully grouped plantings. This attitude persisted through the Victorian era, informing the planning of New York's Central Park in 1856, Philadelphia's Fairmount Park in the 1850's and 1860's, and the Princeton University Campus from 1869 on.

143. Old Convent, St. Paul's Church. Probably erected c. 1880 and later destroyed, this building was representative of the simple form of Tuscan Revival common in New Jersey. Basically it was a traditional rectangular five-bay house, a staple of vernacular building since the mid-eighteenth century. But the cupola and portico marked its Italianate associations.

144. Westland, 15 Hodge Road. Like the convent this is basically a traditional house with a superficial overlay of Italianate brackets and columns. It was built in 1854 for Caroline Stockton Dod and her husband. Grover Cleveland purchased it in 1896 and named it for his friend, Dean Andrew Fleming West.

145. Nassau Hall and the old Chapel. Notman's simple blocky forms and the plainness and lack of ornament of the old Chapel may have suited the college's Calvinistic Presbyterians. Its popish cruciform plan did not. The trustees were so irate that they considered demolishing the partially completed building. But the walls were two-thirds up. Frugality overcame piety and the building was completed as planned.

146. 130 Stockton Street. When Notman was commissioned to design Fieldwood, he found Joseph Olden's mid-eighteenth century stone house standing at the edge of the property. He "Gothicized" it with steep gables, producing a charmingly picturesque lodge.

147. Ivy Hall, 43 Mercer Street. Ivy Hall was built in 1846 to house Princeton's abortive attempt to create a Law School. It subsequently served as the offices of the canal company and the first home of the Ivy Club. It now belongs to Trinity Church. Like the cottage above, this is one of Notman's essays in the Gothic mode, with steeply pitched gables and pointed arches. Though small, it is monumental, composed of the heavy interlocking volumetric shapes that Notman favored.

148. Central Pavilion, Nassau Hall. Next to the cupola and end towers, the most striking features of Notman's Nassau Hall were the powerful, rusticated round-arched door, rising two stories, and the balconied window breaking through the base of the pediment above.

149. Stairway in west tower, Nassau Hall.

150, 151. Stairhall, Guernsey Hall. The optimism and expansiveness of the Victorian era were expressed in the amplitude of architectural scale and the exuberance of space and form. The great rotunda of Guernsey Hall, rising the full height of the building, captures space and sends it spiraling upward with the Baroque curves of the staircase until it bursts through the skylight to mingle with the sky above.

152. Interior, dome, Chancellor Green Library. In the decades following the Civil War all the romantic tendencies of the 1840's and 1850's were heightened. Silhouettes became looser and more irregular. A plethora of ornament, materials, and color freely dissolved sharp outlines, making the parts of a building blend gradually into one another and with their surroundings. In contrast to the single skylight of Guernsey Hall, Chancellor Green's eight stained glass lights cast a broken, shimmering light on the reading room and stacks below. It glittered over a profusion of rich materials—frescoed ceiling, carved wood bookcases, and cast iron columns, which, with gilt flower-bedecked capitals, supported a balcony bounded by a balustrade of gilded filigree.

153. Chancellor Green Library. Under the leadership of James McCosh, who became President in 1868, the College enjoyed a renaissance both intellectual and physical. One of the earliest buildings erected during his administration was this handsome octagonal structure. Designed by William A. Potter, it was completed in 1873. By 1896 it was clearly inadequate as a library and a new building (Pyne) was erected, adjoining it to the south. Chancellor Green was retained as a reading room. After Pyne was replaced by Firestone Library, Chancellor Green became a student center. Although its interior has been stripped of much of its decoration, the exterior remains intact. With its multicolored tile roof, striped stonework, and stained glass, it is a fine example of Venetian Gothic, the style that introduced the polychromatic effects so characteristic of High Victorian architecture.

154. Stuart Hall, Princeton Theological Seminary. Potter was also called upon to play a role in the post-Civil War building activity on the seminary campus. He designed Stuart Hall in 1876, again in Venetian Gothic. If it seems a bit heavy and over-decorated to modern eyes, it was certainly appreciated in its own era. Hageman judged it "the best constructed building in Princeton, as to material and workmanship, and perhaps also as to style and adaptation . . . massive, beautiful and imposing. . . ."

155. Witherspoon Hall. Built in 1877 from plans by R. H. Robertson, Witherspoon Hall is almost a catalogue of High Victorian vices and virtues. The architect seems to have been determined to display his entire repertoire of decorative effects, based on several historic styles, without much regard for their consonance with one another or for their integration into the whole. But the structure is solid, the materials good and well-chosen, and the interior planned for comfort and convenience.

156. Old Marquand Chapel. Before the Civil War, American architects, with a few notable exceptions, lacked formal training. Like Steadman and Notman they were master carpenters whose talent enabled them to transmute the lessons of experience and pattern-books into tasteful and original designs. Richard Morris Hunt was of a new generation. Trained in Paris, at the École des Beaux Arts, he was able to meet his wealthy clients as an educated gentleman among equals. Hunt first arrived in Princeton in company with Henry G. Marquand, donor of the chapel, to look over the site in 1874. The project must have occupied him for several years, as the building was not completed until 1881. In the meantime, he designed Murray Hall, the original Gothic building of what is now Murray-Dodge Hall, the seminary's Lenox Library (now demolished), and two adjoining faculty residences, all built in 1879. The design for Marquand Chapel was freely based on French Romanesque architecture, with which Hunt had undoubtedly become familiar during his sojourn at the Beaux Arts. Massive, strongly articulated, utilizing the stoniness of its material to the full extent, the Chapel was a far cry from the flamboyant châteaux Hunt designed for New York society. It burned in 1920 and was replaced by the present High Gothic building, designed by Cram and Ferguson and dedicated in 1928.

157. The University Hotel. Begun in 1875 and planned by Potter in extravagant Gothic style, with a stick style wooden porch, the University Hotel stood at Nassau Street and University Place on the site of the present dining halls.

158, 159. Alexander Hall, in a lithograph of 1906 and today. William A. Potter's building erected in 1892 was fully appreciated in its own time. Montgomery Schuyler, perhaps the foremost architectural critic America has produced, wrote that it was a "design upon the whole quite worthy of the robust master [Richardson] himself . . . one of the architectural possessions of Princeton, a vigorous, consistent and refined piece of work, carried out, without and within, with an amplitude of means which the artistic skill employed upon them prevents at any point from degenerating into mere ostentation or sumptuosity. An entire college in this manner would not lack interest." Succeeding generations, attuned to the symmetrical coolness of a new classical revival, tended to castigate Alexander Hall. In recent years its importance as an exemplar of Richardsonian Romanesque and as a work of art in its own right are once more being recognized.

160. Detail, arch of ambulatory, Alexander Hall.

161. Detail, doorway, old Art Museum. Combined with the Victorian propensity for using a variety of materials was an affection for and understanding of the intrinsic nature of each individual material. Unlike builders of the classically oriented architecture of the eighteenth and early nineteenth centuries, Victorians would not have thought of sanding wood to make it look like stone, or roughcasting brick with stucco. Instead, as here, they roughened stone to heighten its stoniness, enhancing its solidity by contrast with the more delicate handling of the softer Tiffany brick used for the framing of the arched doorway.

162. Projected Art Museum. Only the central section of this building, designed by A. Page Brown in 1887, was ever erected. In 1921 when larger quarters were needed for the growing Department of Art and Archaeology and the School of Architecture, McCormick Hall, designed by Cram and Ferguson, was added to the west to form an L. The old Art Museum was demolished in 1964. Had it been completed as planned, it would have been a fine example of the style known as Richardsonian Romanesque (after its most eminent practitioner, Henry Hobson Richardson), although it owed as much to the palaces of Renaissance Italy as to the churches of Romanesque France. Still eminently Victorian in its free adaptation of styles of the past, its expansive scale and its rich use of materials, the Art Museum was representative of a style which attempted to clarify structure through the solidity of its forms and the repetition of such motifs as prominent round-arched openings. Ornament might still be lavish and executed with respect for a handicraft tradition which was soon to vanish, but it was never allowed to interfere with the integrity of structural shapes.

163. Reunion Hall. The mansard roof, brought to prominence in Baron Haussmann's rebuilding of Paris during the Second Empire, was a fashionable and eminently practical method of admitting light and air to the garret. Although it became overwhelmingly popular throughout the United States, it was used sparingly on the Princeton campus. Reunion Hall, built in 1870 to celebrate the reunion of the two divisions of the Presbyterian Church, was one of the few new buildings with a mansard roof, and East and West Colleges were reroofed in corresponding fashion. Reunion was demolished in 1966.

164. 12-14 Murray Place. The mansard roof was accepted with enthusiasm for domestic architecture. Underneath it, in this residence built c. 1870, lies the same old five-bay house familiar through two centuries of Princeton architecture, here trans- formed by the roof and the ample porch and enlarged windows, which provided the opportunity for the close communion with nature considered so desirable in the nineteenth century.

165. 16 Stockton Street. Built in 1878 as a manse for the Second Presbyterian Church, it was a simplified version of the more elaborate High Victorian buildings on the college campus. Although the builder used a few boxy structural units, he opened them with a multiplicity of windows of various sizes and shapes, fronting them with the omnipresent porch.

166. 29 University Place. By the early 1870's builders were no longer concerned with conforming to a particular historic style. Here a French mansard roof, striped in a polychromy derived from Venetian Gothic and crowned with vaguely Gothic cast-iron pinnacles, mingles with Italianate brackets and window headings.

167. 79 Alexander Street. Victorian decoration was often applied with great exuberance. The builder of this house used extravagant bargeboards to mask the actual simplicity of the triangular gables.

Domestic building activity in Princeton suffered a hiatus from the mid-1850's through the early 1870's. The financial panic of 1857, the decline in canal traffic, and the moving of the railroad tracks to the Junction brought to an end the town's function as a local center of trade and transportation. Almost totally dependent on its educational institutions, the town languished as the college floundered through the years immediately preceding and following the Civil War. Only when the recovery program under McCosh had restored the college to an eminent position did building activity resume in the town. From 1870-80 new streets, such as University Place (then Railroad Avenue) and Dickinson and Chestnut Streets, were opened. New residences were built along them and along Prospect Avenue and Bayard Lane as well. By 1886 the town was once again depressed and losing population, but in the early 1890's further expansion at the college inaugurated a new burst of building.

168. 32 Wiggins Street

The Victorian pendulum seemed to swing from dependence on historical styles and love of ornament carried to excess to repeatedly renewed cries for a return to truth, reality, and beauty. Towards the end of the nineteenth century one of these periodic movements for reform culminated in the popularity of the so-called Queen Anne style. It bore little resemblance to the architectural style of the reign of the monarch whose name it borrowed, although it utilized occasional motifs like the Palladian window in the gable at 32 Wiggins Street. Rather it expressed in wood the same concern with structural form that was characteristic of the masonry buildings of the Richardsonian Romanesque. At the same time it shared with all the variants of Victorian style a predilection for picturesque massing and an appreciation for ample scale and domestic comfort.

169. 2 Hamilton Avenue

170. Princeton in a lithograph printed in 1874. Fin-de-siècle
Princeton still looked amazingly rural and green. Although the
campus boasted some impressive buildings, and although the
Princeton Press complained equally in 1886 of the dullness of
business and the high price of land which had had the "evil
result [of] the cutting of it into small lots. . . . Hence the
cramped look of our streets . . . ," immediately beyond the
still small cluster at the town's center, cultivated fields and
woodland stretched as far as the eye could see.

IX · ACADEMICISM

In the Late Nineteenth and Early Twentieth Century

IN THE 1880's profound changes took place in American architecture, partly in reaction to what was considered the undisciplined extravagance of High Victorian. This reaction expressed itself in two different directions with a similar aim: to break with the romantic sentimentalism and associationalism of the past and return to simplicity, reality, and purity of form and style. One group sought the answer in an academicism based on the disciplined training received at the École des Beaux Arts. The other group felt that the only road away from Picturesque Eclecticism was a progressivism that grew out of the architecture of Henry Hobson Richardson and was represented by Louis Sullivan and other architects of the Chicago School. The latter took Victorian freedom of interpretation, free-flowing space, undisguised structure, and new advances in technology and combined them into a "modern" architecture in which the bare structure and function of a building were turned into positive aesthetic qualities.

In 1893 the Columbian Exposition at Chicago introduced to the American public a "great white city," modeled after Imperial Roman architecture and embodying the success of Victorian material prosperity. It was the triumph of Beaux Arts academicism, which obscured progressive ideas and dominated the architecture of the country for forty years.

Princeton has no examples of the progressive but many of the academic type of architecture from the late nineteenth and early twentieth centuries. Town and gown seemed to have concurred in their adherence to the conservative. The tenor of the times seems well embodied in one notable Princetonian, Moses Taylor Pyne, and one notable event, the Sesquicentennial celebration, in 1896, of the founding of the College of New Jersey.

Moses Taylor Pyne, a wealthy graduate of the college, 1877, and a trustee from 1885, came to live in Princeton in 1895. He obviously thought of himself as a gentleman in the grand manner of English county society as well as a generous benefactor of the town and college. After buying Drumthwacket, one of the handsomest houses in town, he proceeded to convert it into a large estate with stables and greenhouses built in a medieval style; an extensive park with formal gardens, swans, and peacocks; and a Gothic library inside the house itself. His gift of twin buildings, Upper (Fig. 173) and Lower Pyne, housing both shops and dormitories, brought to Nassau Street a flavor reminiscent of an English country village.

Other men like Pyne, among them Junius Morgan and Archibald Russell, Pyne's brother-in-law, also chose Princeton as the residence most perfectly suited to their tastes; close enough to the city to be convenient but enough removed to be tranquil, at the doorstep of their alma mater, and benefiting from the cultural and intellectual life nurtured by the university. Both Morgan and Russell built elegant houses in the academic tradition and lived on a scale unequaled before in Princeton.

Led by these alumni residents, the town was largely dependent on the college for its livelihood. Infected by the fever of preparation for the Sesquicentennial celebration by the college, it conducted a clean-up campaign which resulted in the founding of a Village Improvement Society and constructed a triumphal arch to be used in the ceremonial procession.

For the college the Sesquicentennial was both a culmination of changes and developments preceding it and a promise of future growth. Professor, later Dean, Andrew F. West, who had been agitating for a true graduate college, was the chief organizer of the celebration. He had gleaned many ideas for the future of the college from his visits to Oxford and Cambridge; and he and his faculty colleagues finally succeeded in persuading the trustees that the college was ready to become a university. Accordingly on October 22, 1896, President Patton announced at the ceremonies that the name of the College of New Jersey was officially changed to Princeton University. Scholars from Cambridge, Trinity College (Dublin), Göttingen, Edinburgh, Leipzig, and Utrecht were invited to lecture, giving an international tone to the event and reinforcing the claim to university status. Princeton's aspirations were well expressed in words by Woodrow Wilson in his famous speech, "Princeton in the Nation's Service." In more tangible form, the college's intention to become an internationally famous university was embodied in the choice of the Collegiate Gothic style of architecture. Moses Taylor Pyne, under the influence of West, who was convinced that architectural emulation of Oxford would produce a similar intellectual climate at the new university, led the trustees' building committee in its choice.

Switching from the Richardsonian Romanesque of Alexander Hall to Tudor Gothic for the Pyne Library in 1897, William Potter concluded his career of more than twenty-five years as one of Princeton's architects. In the next three decades Collegiate Gothic buildings, designed primarily by three firms, almost obliterated the physical imprint of the McCosh era. Cope and Stewardson designed Blair Hall, Blair Gate (Fig. 174), and Stafford Little Hall (Fig. 175), among others. Even those who question the validity of imposing a fifteenth-century English medieval style on a twentieth-century American university must admire their qualities of good proportion, scale, and spatial relationships. A second Philadelphia firm, Day and Klauder, was commissioned over a period of about thirty years to work for the university. Holder (Figs. 181, 182) and Madison Halls are the earliest and most admired of their works. Cram, Goodhue, and Ferguson, of Boston, the most famous exponents of the Late Victorian Gothic Revival in America, built for Princeton the first residential graduate college (Figs. 184, 185) in this country. The isolated site near the golf course was controversial academically but aesthetically felicitous. The gently rolling contours of the land were particularly suited to the Collegiate Gothic, and the architects produced a design successful, within its limitations of style, as a well composed and sited building complex. The strict adherence to archaeological correctness of an architect like Ralph Adams Cram is nowhere more clearly demonstrated than in the University Chapel, built in 1925-28. Cram, like Augustus Welby North Pugin before him in England, was an evangelist of the Gothic Revival, writing profusely on its merits and claiming for it truth, beauty, and realism. Added to his evangelism was a thorough knowledge and understanding of medieval Gothic architecture. Cram was typical of the class of professional architects of his generation. Rich, successful, highly literate and a theoretician as well as designer, he was in every way the peer of his wealthy clients. He ran a large office with many underlings, working on a number of commissions at once. At Princeton he was supervising architect from 1904 to 1927. The standardization imposed on the campus by the exclusive use of Collegiate Gothic was not to be broken until after the Second World War.

During the years immediately preceding the Sesquicentennial of the college, the Morven properties had been broken up; in succeeding years this land was developed as prime residential property along Hodge Road, Boudinot Street, Cleveland Lane, and the extension of Steadman Street into Library Place. Some of the same architects who worked for the college were hired by townspeople to design houses for them in medieval revival styles. Several Tudor half-timber houses of this period can still be seen on Library Place and Cleveland Lane. A late reflection of the Tudor half-timber revival, the faculty houses on Broadmead, was the gift of Moses Taylor Pyne in the 1920's. Constitution Hill (Fig. 177), Junius Morgan's house, and Ivy Club (Fig. 176), one of the college dining clubs on Prospect Avenue, were both essays in Tudor Gothic by Cope and Stewardson. Thus for a time the relatively modest forms of Steadman's classic revival were eclipsed by the more ambitious Victorian devotion to medieval revivals.

A second aspect of Late Victorian academicism, the Colonial Revival, was initiated in the work of the New York firm of McKim, Mead and White. Trained in Richardson's atelier, Charles Follen McKim and Stanford White later joined with William Mead to form one of the most successful firms of the day. The three made a walking tour of New England in 1877 that convinced them of the virtues of colonial architecture. The colonial became their chief style for domestic building. For their monumental designs, however, they usually chose Imperial Roman, the mode in which as chief architects they designed for the Chicago World's Fair. While the medieval revival dominated the college campus in the late nineteenth and early twentieth centuries, the colonial became more important for the town. For Cottage Club (Fig. 179), on Prospect Avenue, McKim, Mead and White designed a brick mansion in the Georgian mode. William Stone, a lesser known New Yorker who designed in colonial as well as other styles, was a favored architect for people about to move into the new streets behind Morven. Princeton has one unusual and outstanding example of Dutch Revival by Stone, the old Princeton Bank and Trust Company building (Fig. 171) at 12 Nassau Street. Of this building Montgomery Schuyler wrote, "Of the many buildings which have been suggested by that famous and fantastic old sixteenth-century meat market of Haarlem, none is more successful or seems more in place than this."

Of all the Late Victorian revivals, the colonial was the most persistent in the town of Princeton, continuing to dominate the scene until after World War II. The Westminster Choir College, Fuld Hall (Fig. 186) at the Institute for Advanced Study, and Palmer Square all testify to the strength of this devotion. Palmer Square (Fig. 187) was conceived by Edgar Palmer, a wealthy graduate of the university who had come to Princeton to live, like Moses Taylor Pyne a generation before, and devoted much of his interest and money to the town. Originally the square was intended to be a civic center, providing shops and open space for pedestrians and eliminating some slum conditions nearby. As executed, the plan is incomplete but has the merits of good proportions, human scale, and a modicum of variety within the chosen style limitation. One hopes that if Palmer Square were built today there would be more regard for the preservation of genuine eighteenth- and nineteenth-century buildings, less re-creation of a colonial Princeton that never existed, and an attempt to produce a design relevant to twentieth-century American life.

171. Old Princeton Bank and Trust Building, 12 Nassau Street. Until the end of the nineteenth century and through the first three decades of the twentieth, Princeton's buildings, like the majority of American buildings, continued unbroken the Victorian tradition of dependence on styles of the past. Indeed, the practice is still very much alive. One addition to the repertoire was the revival of styles from America's own past, particularly Georgian and New England and Dutch Colonial. An especially successful example of the last is the old Princeton Bank and Trust, designed by W. E. Stone in 1896, now occupied by offices and stores.

172. Nassau Street c. 1915. When this photograph was made, the new Gothic construction was beginning to transform the Princeton skyline. Holder Tower, to the right in the picture, and Cleveland Tower at the Graduate College rose high above the cupola of Nassau Hall, which had dominated the town for so long. Nassau Street, however, was still the wide, dusty main street of a small town, traversed by horse-drawn vehicles. The sign at the left was one of the few forecasts of approaching change.

173. Upper Pyne, 74-76 Nassau Street. Moses Taylor Pyne's dream of a university based on English prototypes was complemented by a vision of Nassau Street as the high street of an English village. Accordingly, in 1896 he commissioned Raleigh C. Gildersleeve to produce two half-timbered dormitories. Lower Pyne still stands at 92 Nassau Street. Upper Pyne was demolished in 1964.

175. Stafford Little Hall, erected in 1899 southwest of Blair Hall, was designed by Cope and Stewardson, to harmonize with their preceding work.

174. Blair Tower. The decision of the trustees, in 1896, that henceforth the university's architecture would conform to the English Gothic style was implemented rapidly. Among the first of the new buildings was Blair Hall, built in 1897 and designed by the firm of Walter Cope and John Stewardson.

176. Ivy Club, 43 Prospect Avenue. Here, in 1897, Cope and Stewardson chose a Tudor Gothic, somewhat more restrained than the battlemented style of their campus buildings.

177. Constitution Hill. In 1896 Junius Morgan purchased the Constitution Hill property and demolished Robert Stockton's pre-Revolutionary farmhouse (Fig. 23). He used the site for this baronial Tudor mansion designed by Cope and Stewardson.

178. Detail, McCosh House, 381 Nassau Street. When President McCosh retired in 1887 he moved to a house that had been built for him on Prospect Avenue. It was moved to its present location in 1894. It was one of Princeton's earliest domestic essays in the Colonial Revival, which was the last in the long series of Victorian revivals and the one whose impact, after eighty years, seems as strong in Princeton as ever. The same interest in the expression of the structural qualities of materials that had led the late Victorians to acceptance of the Richardsonian Romanesque and the variants of Queen Anne also brought them to a serious consideration of the structural nature of early American architecture. Besides, our own history was now remote enough to be looked on with nostalgia, and the celebration of the centennial in 1876 had awakened interest in the nation's past. So the Scottish-born McCosh retired to a house assembled from a repertoire of Georgian motifs, most of which, like this window, were far more elaborate than anything to be seen in eighteenth-century Princeton.

179. Cottage Club, 51 Prospect Avenue. As young draftsmen in the office of H. H. Richardson, Charles McKim and Stanford White made a walking tour of New England which awakened in both an interest in early American building. Although their public style favored the Renaissance and Imperial Rome, their domestic designs (and Cottage Club, built in 1904, is no larger than the mansions of some of their wealthy clients) often reflected Colonial and Georgian precedents.

180. FitzRandolph Gateway. In 1905 the iron fence which had adorned the front campus since 1838 was taken down and a triumphal gateway, designed by McKim, Mead and White, was installed in its place. A free adaptation of Georgian ironwork, it brought back to campus the motif of urns, which had decorated the first college wall in the eighteenth century, adding to them a pair of imperial eagles, like those surmounting New York City's recently demolished Pennsylvania Station.

181. Court, Madison and Holder Halls.

In 1915 the old University Hotel (Fig. 157), which had long ceased to function as a hostelry and become a somewhat inadequate dormitory and commons, was torn down. In its place were erected the present university dining halls, Holder in 1910 and Madison in 1916. Their architects, Day and Klauder, were typical of the new generation. Impatient with the eclectic intermingling of styles of the High Victorian era, they nevertheless shared the Victorian hope of evoking past excellence through an association with period architecture. But they did so with a passion for authenticity that was new. Each style was re-examined in the light of the archaeological knowledge that had been systematically assembled during the nineteenth century. Their ornament was true to period prototypes; to insure its hand-crafted appearance, in an America which was rapidly becoming totally industrialized, skilled stonecutters were brought from Italy.

182. Cloister, Holder Hall.

183. Whig and Clio Halls. In 1889 the old Halls (Figs. 117, 118), which had been erected in 1838, were demolished, and work was begun on new buildings designed by A. Page Brown. These, completed in 1893, were placed somewhat closer together than their predecessors. They were, in effect, copies of copies, reproducing in marble and on a grander scale the earlier wood-trimmed stucco Greek Revival structures. Their proportion and detail may have been closer to antique prototypes; certainly their material was. But their academic severity resulted in a cold hardness, far less appealing than the original translation of Greek vocabulary into small scale and native materials.

184. The Graduate College, archway leading to Thomson Court.

The foremost advocate of the archaeological Gothic Revival of the early twentieth century was Ralph Adams Cram of Boston. As supervising architect of the university from 1904 to 1927 he presided over the transformation of the campus into a monument to the Collegiate Gothic style. Although other firms, notably Day and Klauder, designed many of Princeton's buildings, his own firm was responsible for the design of the Uni-

versity Chapel, completed in 1928, and the Graduate College, completed in 1913. In the hands of an architect like Cram, the Collegiate Gothic, carefully constructed of the best materials, beautifully sited, achieved great charm and even distinction. Whether medieval cloisters provided a suitable setting for young men preparing to cope with twentieth-century realities "in the Nation's service" is less certain.

185. The Graduate College, Cleveland Tower.

186. Fuld Hall, Institute for Advanced Study. The Institute was founded in 1930 to provide a unique environment for scholars, in which they might pursue their studies free from the responsibilities of teaching or imposed schedules. Unfortunately the originality and magnitude of this concept was not approached in the original physical plant. Fuld Hall, designed by Jens Fredrick Larson, is a particularly sterile example of neo-Georgian, representing the popular taste of the 1930's in its least inspired form.

187. Palmer Square. By 1936 when Palmer Square, designed by Thomas Stapleton, was begun, the use of Colonial Revival for the small town civic center the Square was originally conceived to be was almost a foregone conclusion. The nostalgia for an earlier, simpler, and seemingly better America had been reenforced by the uncertainties of the Depression. Besides, the opening of the American Wing of the Metropolitan Museum of Art and the development of Colonial Williamsburg in the 1920's had given the style the official stamp of artistic respectability. The shops along the west side of Palmer Square are a particularly happy result of the vogue for "authentic" reproduction. Their intimate scale, large windows and sheltering bays, arcades, and balconies invite the pedestrian to tarry and browse in a manner especially attractive in an era when the overwhelming automobile threatens to banish the pedestrian from the streets of most towns.

X · THE TWENTIETH CENTURY

I<small>N</small> April of 1921 Moses Taylor Pyne died. After services at Drumthwacket an elaborate cortege wound its way up Stockton Street, through the graduate college, around Nassau Hall, and finally to the cemetery. Bare-headed students formed an honor guard along the route. It was an impressive funeral for the benefactor of town and college. In May of the same year, Albert Einstein, who had been invited to lecture at Princeton for the first time, was honored by a formal academic procession; alumni were invited to appear in academic robes along with faculty. These two events, the funeral of Moses Taylor Pyne and the visit of Albert Einstein, are symbolic of the end of one era and the beginning of another.

The changes in Princeton from that time to the present affected the character of both the town and the university. Although the first signs of these changes occurred in the thirties, the effects were not noticeable until after the Second World War. Between the two world wars Princeton remained a quiet college town relatively unaffected by the social and economic upheavals experienced elsewhere, but the founding of the Institute for Advanced Study in 1930 and the appointment of Einstein as its first professor in 1932 presaged a less parochial future. From its inception the Institute was international in outlook, personnel, and repute. Its arrival indicated the eventual end to the hegemony of university and seminary in the intellectual field. In 1935 the American Institute of Public Opinion, popularly known as the Gallup Poll, made its headquarters in Princeton, a harbinger of a different kind of institution that the town would continue to attract in the decades to come. Still another nationally important organization, Educational Testing Service, made Princeton its home in 1948.

Immediately after World War II, Radio Corporation of America opened its David Sarnoff Laboratories in Penns Neck. Other companies followed; Western Electric, Food Machinery Corporation, the Textile Research Institute, and various electronics firms. The arrival of these firms and the increase of government sponsored research at the university has changed Princeton from a small residential college town to a center of industrial and scientific research. The dramatic rate of growth of Princeton as a suburb in post-war America has also altered its character. The town is becoming, willingly or not, part of the sprawling megalopolis radiating from New York. In the decade from 1950 to 1960 the population of Princeton Township doubled. In the peak year 1956 there were 1000 buildings of various types and sizes going up in the Borough and Township.

The building boom of the 1950's offered a great opportunity to produce significant contemporary architecture, but like most other small towns in the United States, Princeton was too conservative to profit from it. The result has been a series of overpriced housing developments that are completely derivative of Late Victorian colonial revivals. Frequently the builders of these houses have given their clients the benefit of a contemporary open floor plan, but have then masked it with a neo-colonial exterior. The ubiquitous ranch house is a weak bow to Frank Lloyd Wright, with no understanding of his handling of materials or basic ideas of design. One exception to the colonial mania, the Clover Lane-Deerpath group of houses, was a successful effort to provide moderately priced, functional houses in a frankly modern idiom.

After a twenty-five year hiatus in building on the campus, the university found itself in desperate need of new physical facilities immediately after World War II. Continuing to think in the same mold as it had under the guidance of Ralph Adams Cram, it began construction in 1946 of a vast $10 million library that was to have a completely up-to-date interior but preserve a pseudo-collegiate Gothic exterior. It was the last gasp of this style on the college campus. Following its completion, the university concluded that Gothic construction was no longer feasible.

The history of the emergence and subsequent development of modern architecture in the United States is complex. From an auspicious beginning in the late nineteenth and early twentieth centuries in work of the Chicago School, particularly that of Frank Lloyd Wright, and in California with Maybeck, Gill, and the Greenes, it sank into oblivion for about twenty years. During this period, just before and after World War I, the exciting developments in architecture were taking place in Europe, in the Bauhaus group in Germany; in the De Stijl group in Holland; and in the work of Le Corbusier in France. While Late Victorian architects had used modern technological innovations but had hidden them under traditional forms, these European avant-garde architects, anxious to make a complete break with the past, created an architecture in which structural and functional elements were the principal aesthetic features of the design. The possibilities of the machine age were freely exploited not only in architecture but in painting, sculpture, and industrial design as well. Structure and function were emphasized, ornament was eliminated, rectilinear shapes were favored, surfaces were smooth. The common use of the steel frame skeleton, by eliminating the need for supporting walls, enabled architects to treat space differently. Enclosed only by large expanses of glass and thin metal strips or panels, it was treated as a constantly changing shifting element, interrupted and punctuated by partitions but interpenetrating between interior and exterior. Just as Cubist painters fragmented space into visual planes on the surface of a painting, the architects of the International Style broke up the volumes of space within their buildings.

It was not until after the depression of 1929 that this kind of modern architecture began to appear in America, as an importation brought over by refugees. Ignored in the United States, the ideas of Frank Lloyd Wright had been assimilated by these International Style architects, who were the leaders of the modern movement of the thirties in the United States. Walter Gropius and Marcel Breuer came to Harvard from the Bauhaus in 1937; Mies van der Rohe, Gropius' successor at the Bauhaus, arrived at the Illinois Institute of Technology in 1938. These foreign-born architects trained the young Americans who became our leading designers of the fifties and sixties. Frank Lloyd Wright, whose star began to rise again in the thirties, created and conducted a school of his own, but while his work has been tremendously influential in modern design, he did not have a host of trained disciples to carry on his work. However, Wright's individualistic ideas were important for the generation following Gropius, Mies, and Breuer.

In the thirties a few enlightened patrons were primarily responsible for the concrete realization of designs by the émigré architects. The impetus toward fuller acceptance of modern architecture in the United States was a reaction against the old order, caused by the depression of 1929 and the disillusionment following World War II. Immediately after 1945, freed from the inhibiting effect of the war, businesses, industries, and public institutions launched extensive building programs which have continued unabated to the present. Commissions were given to architects of the new school. Among the leaders in the educational field to give commissions to recognized architects of the modern movement were Harvard (Graduate Center, Gropius with Architects Collaborative, 1949), Massachusetts Institute of Technology (Dormitory, Alvar Aalto, 1949), Illinois Institute of Technology (campus plan, Mies van der Rohe, 1939-1952).

In Princeton, one of the earliest adventures into modern design was the housing project of the Institute for Advanced Study (Fig. 189) planned by Marcel Breuer (1957) as garden apartments for visiting fellows. Working with simple rectangular modules, the architect provided flexibility in the size of the units and variety in their arrangement, while maintaining a functional design. Built of red brick with wood trim, the apartments have been placed to take advantage of the park-like setting; large expanses of glass enable the occupants to enjoy the surrounding landscape. In 1964 the Institute continued its policy of hiring distinguished architects by commissioning the firm of Harrison and Abramowitz to do a new library (Fig. 191). It combines classic simplicity of line, again with the emphasis on rectilinear shapes and with elegance in the use of materials. The finely finished wood panels set in angular patterns relieve the starkness of the white roof and present a foil to the transparent glass walls. Natural light, diffused and baffled by white cement coves, enters the roof through a series of clerestory windows.

In 1959 Princeton University embarked on a $53 million fund-raising campaign that was to result in a major building program on the campus. The Collegiate Gothic style was finally abandoned in favor of contemporary design. As expressed by Douglas Orr, the supervising architect of this program, the guiding principle was the subordination of the designs of the individual buildings to the park-like atmosphere so characteristic of the campus. Nature was to rule over structure in an attempt to harmonize the old with the new. While in theory this seemed to be a sound precept, in practice it fostered unevenness in quality and militated against innovations in the modern

179

idiom. In trying to please all, it satisfied none, neither the sentimentalists who wished to continue Collegiate Gothic nor those who looked for buildings expressive of a modern university. The Engineering Quadrangle is neither an evocation of a past style nor a clear statement of modern principles of design and construction. Its monotonous expanses of glass and brick mask the structural elements of the building and fail to articulate or unify the façades. At McCormick Hall the difficulty of incorporating the neo-Venetian Renaissance wing of a forty-year-old building into the new construction has resulted in a non-functional structure in which teaching, research, and study have not been conveniently coordinated. On the exterior, vertical pink stone panels punctuated with thin glass strips promise monumentality and a sense of dignity that is not fulfilled in the execution. Far more successful within the prescribed formula is the Architecture Building, in which the alternation of large glass panels and projecting brick bays over a raised glass basement makes the walls seem to float. The reflecting possibilities of glass are realized especially around the entrance pavilion.

Perhaps in an effort to placate the modernists, the university modified its approach to architectural design and engaged Minoru Yamasaki to design the new building for the Woodrow Wilson School of Public and International Affairs (Figs. 193, 194; 1965). It rises at the corner of Prospect Avenue and Washington Road, a gleaming contrast to its sober grey neighbors. Yamasaki's obvious reference in this building to the Parthenon and the Ducal Palace in Venice may be his way of recalling historical tradition while still designing in modern terms. The colonnade surrounding the building, while intentionally reminiscent of a Greek peristyle temple, is cast in modern forms and makes use of modern construction techniques.

In one of the conspicuously successful buildings on the campus, the dormitory complex designed by the firm of Hugh Stubbins Associates, the architect has related a contemporary design to its predecessors without compromising its style. The grey brick and concrete harmonize with the grey stone of Collegiate Gothic, the scale echoes its neighbors, and the spatial relationships of the quadrangle recall others on campus. A skillful use of apparently shifting planes gives a dynamic quality to the silhouette. With this, other recent buildings, and the completion of the astro-physics and the mathematics tower complex, the university approaches the end of its mid-twentieth-century building program. Princeton's timidity and confusion in visual expression seems incompatible with its leadership in education.

As the university has been struggling to solve its architectural problems, the town, in a more haphazard way, has been doing the same. Throughout the fifties and sixties a few private homes of modern design have been built. Some of the most distinctive were designed for the architect's own use, among them Robert Engelbrecht's at 145 Mansgrove Road, the late Kenneth Kassler's at 32 Lafayette Road West (Fig. 188), and Robert Geddes' at the corner of Mercer Street and Lovers Lane. The Engelbrecht house displays technological ingenuity and aesthetic sensibility in adapting a design to a difficult site. The Geddes house proves that a relatively standard "in-town" lot need be no barrier to originality. This house makes a powerful impression through its strong, almost brutal, alternation of mass and void and its arrangement of isolated pavilions around a central core.

Three public institutions in Princeton have recently ventured into the modern field. In Stuart Country Day School (Fig. 190), designed by Jean Labatut, functionalism of plan has been combined with interest in texture and color, and a particular desire to incorporate into the building some of the character of the immediate natural sur-roundings. The opportunity of planning an entire educational complex has been seized with a vigor and excitement missing in the banal design of Stuart's neighbor and near-contemporary, the Princeton Day Schools.

When the Princeton Borough Board of Education decided to build the John Witherspoon School for its elementary and junior high school students, it had the foresight and imagination to choose as architect Ernest J. Kump, a well-known spe-cialist in school design. In accord with recent concepts he arranged the classrooms as pavilions around a central core of library, cafeteria, and gymnasium, providing easy access to commonly used facilities but separating age groups. The copper mansard roofs and projecting bay windows are reminiscent of these recurrent motifs in Vic-torian architecture, but there is nothing imitative or derivative about these references to the past. The new public library at the corner of Witherspoon and Wiggins Streets should be further encouragement to civic authorities to seek distinctive modern designs for public buildings.

Despite these recent essays in genuine expressions of twentieth-century needs, both town and gown have been hesitant in accepting the forms of modern architecture. Princeton's traditional conservatism still dominates, at least in the field of the visual arts. It remains to be seen whether Princeton will in fact move with the times or con-tinue to seek refuge in outworn symbols and styles of the past.

188. 32 Lafayette Road West. This house was built by the architect Kenneth Kassler for his own use in 1954. Conforming admirably to the contours of the site, free and open in plan, composed of rugged materials, it is a modern interpretation of a long American tradition of architecture seen as growing naturally from its surroundings, function, and materials. First expressed as conscious theory by A. J. Downing and never totally suppressed even during the height of Victorian eclecticism, this naturalistic strain was imbued with new vigor at the turn of the century by the theory and practice of Louis Sullivan and Frank Lloyd Wright. Its impact on American architecture in general was slight, however, until after World War II.

189. Fellows' Housing, Institute for Advanced Study. The first large-scale Princeton commission in a frankly modern idiom was given to Marcel Breuer, one of the best-known of the European architects who, immigrating to the United States in the 1930's, brought with them a commitment to the principles of the so-called International Style. Stripped to essentials, the buildings depend for their effect on the stark clarity of the patterns formed by the structural members.

190. Stuart Country Day School, The Great Road. Located in the rocky wooded hills of the northwest section of Princeton Township, the craggy forms of Jean Labatut's buildings, completed in 1963, reflect the rugged beauty of their site. The sinuous contours reiterate those of the land. Roughened concrete and green-glazed brick echo the shapes, colors, and texture of boulders and trees. At the same time this rather romantic relation to nature is tempered and controlled by the repeated rhythms of posts, girders, and windows.

191. Library, Institute for Advanced Study. In the 1960's architects have increasingly turned away from the rigid geometry of the International Style. The interrelation of repeated rectangular forms is still the dominating factor in the Library, designed by Harrison and Abramowitz and opened in 1965. But its serene regularity is modified and softened by a sensuous delight in the richness of the materials and the lively contrasts of color and texture.

192. Lourie-Love and 1922 Halls. In planning the university's
new dormitory complex, completed in 1964, which also includes Class of 1940, 1941, and 1942 Halls, Hugh Stubbins
has designed a group of buildings that complements Princeton's
traditional architecture while making a strong statement in
modern terms. Responsive to the Collegiate Gothic in color
and in the rhythm of bay and wall surface, of verticals and
horizontals, the buildings employ straightforward modern materials and construction to achieve their effect.

193. Woodrow Wilson School. A new classicism, personalized and executed with an extreme refinement of proportion and line, characterizes the work of Minoru Yamasaki. Serene and elegant, this building, completed in 1965, provides a fitting culmination to what has long been a main axis of the campus, the tree-arched vista of McCosh Walk.

194. Colonnade, Woodrow Wilson School.

SOME FREQUENTLY USED ARCHITECTURAL TERMS

This brief guide is not intended to be comprehensive or definitive. Many of the words and phrases cited here have been used with somewhat different meanings in other eras, other places, and other disciplines.

Adamesque: Based on the ornate, but delicate, style of the British brothers John (1721-1792) and Robert (1728-1792) Adam.

Ambulatory: A corridor or similar place for walking, usually adjoining a church.

Anthemion: A form of decoration based on the honeysuckle flower and leaves, used extensively in classical antiquity.

Architrave: A molded frame surrounding a door or window: lowest part of an entablature (see Orders).

Barge-boards: Woodwork covering the joint between gable wall and roofing material.

Battlement: A parapet with open spaces.

Bay: A vertical section of a building, usually marked by some structural feature such as a window or columns.

Beaded Siding: Clapboarding on which a rounded edge has been carved or applied.

Bracket: A synonym for console; a projecting support (see also modillion).

Castellated: Having battlements (see above) like a castle.

Chancel: That part of a church reserved for the clergy and choir.

Cinquefoil: Form of tracery having five arcs separated by cusps.

Corinthian: See Orders.

Cornice: Projecting course of wood or masonry at the top of a building or at the joint between a rectangular wall and the roof; interior, molding covering angle formed by wall and ceiling.

Course: Horizontal row of bricks, tiles, stone, etc.

Crocket: Small, carved, decorated projection used to ornament the angles of roofs or spires.

Cusped arches: Arches in which points are formed where curved forms converge.

Dentils: Projecting, small, rectangular blocks (like teeth) used in series as part of ornamentation of a cornice or molding.

Doric: See Orders.

Dormer: Window projecting from a slanting roof.

Finial: Ornament topping a spire or gable; any crowning ornamental detail.

Five-bay house: House with a façade divided into five vertical sections, usually by placing of windows.

Flemish bond: A pattern of bricks laid with headers and stretchers alternating in the same course.

Gable: Triangular wall at end of building formed by angle of slanting roof.

Gallery: Upper story for seats attached to one or more side walls of a church or other public building.

Gouging: Decorative pattern incised with a chisel with a concavo-convex cross-section.

Half-timber construction: Form of construction using a frame of heavy timbers, cross-braced, with the spaces between the framework filled with brick or other material.

Ionic: See Orders.

Light: Any opening in a building constructed for the purpose of admitting light, usually a window.

Lintel: Horizontal member, supported at each end and capable of bearing weight; particularly the horizontal member over a door or window opening. Keyed lintel: A lintel in the form of a flat arch with a wedge-shaped block in the center.

Mansard roof: A roof with a double pitch, often on all four sides, the lower slope being steeper than the upper; a roof steeply pitched on all four sides, with a flat top.

Modillion: Simple curved bracket supporting upper part of a cornice, derived from the Corinthian order.

Muntins: Relatively narrow members dividing, and holding in place, the individual panes of a window or other light.

Oculus: Opening or light in the form of a circle.

Orders: Styles of building, derived from classical antiquity, based on the arrangement and decoration of column and entablature (the horizontal member borne on the columns). Within each order many variations are possible. The descriptions given below are of elements generally found in each order.

Doric: A Greek Doric column has no base, as opposed to the Roman Doric which has a small one. The column's shaft is unfluted and the capital, placed directly on the shaft, is simple and blocky.

Ionic: An Ionic column has a molded base, fluted shaft, and a capital with graceful curved volutes.

Corinthian: A Corinthian column has a molded base, and elaborate capital, with carving usually based on leaf-forms. The shaft of a Greek Corinthian column is fluted; that of a Roman, unfluted.

Tuscan: A Roman order, modified from the Doric, with molded base, unfluted shaft, and capital set off from the shaft by a band, called necking.

Palladian window: Three-light window with an arched central window rising above two narrower side-lights.

Parapet: Protective wall at the edge of a roof, platform or balcony.

Pavilion: Section, projecting, or otherwise distinguished, from the main mass of a building.

Pediment: Triangular area, usually decorated with sculpture or moldings, used to finish the gable end of a classical building, or over a portico, window, or door.

Pilaster: Upright member, attached to a wall, rectangular in section, but treated like a column with base, shaft and capital.

Podium: High platform, approached by stairs on one side, derived from Roman temple form.

Reeding: Delicate convex molding, reverse of fluting.

Segmental arch: Arch in which the contour is a segment of a circle.

Stringcourse: Continuous horizontal band, projecting from the plane of a wall, often marking the division between storys.

Three-bay house: House with a façade divided into three vertical sections, usually by the placing of windows.

Tuscan: See Orders.

Venetian window: Three-light window, in which the central rectangular light is the same height as the two narrower rectangular side-lights.

Watertable: A projecting band around the base of a wall, often with a curved upper course, intended to throw off water.

A NOTE ON SOURCES

For a book of this nature such pictorial records as old photographs, drawings, prints, and paintings are as important as written records. They provide the most direct evidence available of the appearance of a building at a given period in its history. Fortunately a large quantity of pictorial material on Princeton has been preserved. In addition to the examples appearing in this book, a voluminous store is housed in the Department of Rare Books and Special Collections of the Princeton University Library. Of particular importance are a file of photographs on the Borough of Princeton, the Albridge C. Smith Collection of views of Nassau Hall and the university campus, and an unfiled collection of glass-plate negatives from the firm of R. H. Rose & Son, photographers who were active in Princeton from 1874 until the mid-1930's.

The Archives of Princeton University contain much pictorial material, with emphasis on the campus, although early views of buildings and scenes in the town are also represented, particularly in the extensive collection of senior yearbooks, some dating from the 1860's.

While the bulk of material is in these collections, valuable pictorial records not available elsewhere may be found in the Speer Library, Princeton Theological Seminary; the Special Collections of the Rutgers University Library; the Historical Society of Princeton; and private collections in Princeton, notably those of Frederick S. Osborne and Edmund D. Cook & Co. For its bicentennial celebration the First Presbyterian Church assembled a noteworthy group of early views of its successive church buildings and parsonages.

Early maps were useful in pinpointing the locations of buildings. Particularly important for judging early routes through Princeton and the site of Henry Greenland's house are the Reid map of 1685 in the New Jersey Historical Society (published in Whitehead, "East Jersey Under the Proprietary Governments," *Collections of the New Jersey Historical Society*, I) and the Worlidge map, published in London about 1690, in the Library of Congress (published in Pomfret, *The Province of East Jersey, 1609-1702, The Rebellious Proprietary*). Another useful map for determining early boundaries is a survey drawn by William Emley in 1709 (published in Hageman, *Princeton and Its Institutions*, I). Eighteenth-century maps include John Dalley's survey of 1745 in the New-York Historical Society. In the Princeton University Library are Bancker's 1762 copy of the Dalley map; Azariah Dunham's 1766 "Map of the Division line Between the Counties of Middlesex and Somerset"; a series of maps drawn by Louis-Alexandre Berthier, a cartographer with Rochambeau's army; and a road map from "The Traveller's Directory," 1804 (all published, with the exception of No. 24, Sheet 23 of the Berthier papers, in *New Jersey Road Maps of the 18th Century*, Howard C. Rice, ed.). The so-called "spy map" in the Library of Congress (published in Bill, *The Campaign of Princeton, 1776-1777*) shows the no-longer extant back road taken by

Washington's troops, the position of British fortifications and the location of some buildings. A sketch-map of the town in 1784 is in the manuscript of the *Itineraries* of Ezra Stiles at Yale University. The Map Room of the Princeton University Library contains maps of Princeton from the mid-nineteenth through the early years of the twentieth century, with a check-list.

No study of any segment of early New Jersey history could be undertaken without reference to the invaluable source material published in the *New Jersey Archives*. In particular, the newspaper advertisements of real estate for sale contain important information on the early condition of properties.

The richest store of unpublished manuscript sources for the Princeton area is in the Princeton University Library. The majority of these can be readily located through the use of the card catalogue in the Department of Rare Books and Special Collections, although some valuable material on loan to the library in the "temporary deposit" of Stockton papers has not been catalogued. Among the most useful items in Rare Books are numerous letters; a few early deeds not recorded elsewhere; receipted bills, particularly those for work done to buildings and grounds; Nathaniel FitzRandolph's record book; Col. George Morgan's account books; the Peters papers, containing genealogical information, particularly on the Clark and Olden families, and some photographs; reports of early road surveys; and the manuscript of *A Breif Narrative of the Ravages committed by the Regular and Hessian Soldiers*. . . .

The Princeton University Archives contain a wealth of material including the minutes of the board of trustees of the college; biographical data on alumni; the notebooks of V. Lansing Collins, and his annotated copies of Hageman, *Princeton and Its Institutions* and the 1931 edition of *Princeton Past and Present*.

A continuous series of Princeton newspapers from 1832 on, published under several names, is filed in the microfilm room of the Princeton University Library under the name of *The Princeton Packet*. The newspapers contain data not always available elsewhere on building activity, builders, and architects.

In Speer Library at the Princeton Theological Seminary are the minutes of the directors of the seminary. The records of the First Presbyterian Church, including floor plans of all three buildings on the site, are also deposited in Speer Library, in the Synod of New Jersey Collection.

Trinity Church records are in the offices of Trinity Church. The Trenton Free Public Library has, on microfilm, the minutes of the Chesterfield Meeting (of The Society of Friends at Crosswicks), which contain valuable records of the Stony Brook Meeting.

Also in Trenton, The Bureau of Archives and History at the New Jersey State Library contains miscellaneous manuscripts such as the petition for the building of a barracks in Princeton and the petition for creating the Borough of Princeton; Trenton newspapers from 1778-1918, indexed for vital statistics; records of claims for damage done by the British during the Revolutionary War; wills and inventories through the early nineteenth century; and pre-Revolutionary deed books, with some entries up to 1800.

Deeds from 1784 to 1837 are in the Somerset County Administration Building in Somerville and the Middlesex County Courthouse in New Brunswick.

County records, including deeds, from 1838 on are in the Mercer County Courthouse in Trenton.

BIBLIOGRAPHY

Alexander, James W., *The Life of Archibald Alexander, D.D.*, New York, Charles Scribner, 1854

Andrews, Wayne, *Architecture, Ambition, and Americans*, New York, Harper and Bros., 1955

Beam, Jacob Newton, *The American Whig Society of Princeton University*, Princeton, The Society, 1933

Benjamin, Asher, *The American Builder's Companion*, Boston, Etheridge and Bliss, 1806

——, *The Builder's Guide*, Boston, Perkins and Marvin, 1839

——, *The Practical House Carpenter*, Boston, R. P. and C. Williams, and Annin and Smith, 1830; in 1841 and later editions called *The Architect*; fourteen editions to 1857

Biddle, Owen, *The Young Carpenter's Assistant*, Philadelphia, Benjamin Johnson, 1805

—— and John Haviland, *An Improved and Enlarged Edition of Biddle's The Young Carpenter's Assistant*, Philadelphia, McCarty and Davis, 1837

Bill, Alfred Hoyt, *A House Called Morven*, Princeton, Princeton University Press, 1954

——, *The Campaign of Princeton, 1776-1777*, Princeton, Princeton University Press, 1948

Black, William Nelson, "Colonial Building in New Jersey," *Architectural Record*, Jan.-Mar. 1894, III, 245-262

Burchard, John and Albert Bush-Brown, *The Architecture of America*, Boston, Little Brown & Co., 1961

Burnaby, Andrew, *Travels Through the Middle Settlements in North America*, 2d ed., Ithaca, Cornell University Press, 1960

Butterfield, Lyman H., "Morven: A Colonial Outpost of Sensibility, with some hitherto unpublished Poems by Annis Boudinot Stockton," *Princeton University Library Chronicle*, Nov. 1944, VI, 1-16

Chastellux, Marquis de, *Travels in North America*, 2 vols., edited by Howard C. Rice, Jr., Chapel Hill, University of North Carolina Press, 1963

Collins, V. Lansing, editor, *A Brief Narrative of the Ravages of the British and Hessians at Princeton in 1776-77*, Princeton, Princeton Historical Association, 1906

——, *President Witherspoon*, 2 vols., Princeton, Princeton University Press, 1925

——, *Princeton Past and Present*, Princeton, Princeton University Press, 1931, 1945

Condit, Carl W., *The Chicago School of Architecture*, Chicago, University of Chicago Press, 1964

Coolidge, John, *Mill and Mansion*, New York, Columbia University Press, 1942

Dankers, Jasper and Peter Sluyter, *Journal of a Voyage to New York and a Tour in Several of the American Colonies in 1679-80*, Memoirs of the Long Island Historical Society, Brooklyn, 1867

Deane, Silas, *Correspondence*, Connecticut Historical Society Collections, II, Hartford, 1870

Downing, Andrew Jackson, *A Treatise on the Theory and Practice of Landscape Gardening Adapted to North America*, New York and London, Wiley & Putnam, 1841

Downing, Antoinette and Vincent J. Scully, Jr., *The Architectural Heritage of Newport, R.I.*, Cambridge, Harvard University Press, 1952

Eberlein, Harold Donaldson, *Manor Houses and Historic Homes of Long Island and Staten Island*, Philadelphia, J. B. Lippincott, 1928

——, *The Architecture of Colonial America*, Boston, Little Brown, 1915

Egbert, Donald Drew, "General Mercer at the Battle of Princeton as Painted by James Peale, Charles Willson Peale and William Mercer," *Princeton University Library Chronicle*, Summer 1952, XIII, 171-194

——, "The Architecture and Setting," in *The Modern Princeton*, Princeton, Princeton University Press, 1947

Ewan, N. R., *Early Brickmaking in the Colonies*, Camden, Camden County Historical Society, 1938 (reprinted from the *West Jersey Press*)

Freedgood, Seymour, "Life in Princeton," *Fortune*, Dec. 1961, LXIV, 2, 106-110, 221-226

Gibbs, James, *A Book of Architecture*, London, 1728

Giedion, Siegfried, *Space, Time, and Architecture*, Cambridge, Harvard University Press, 1941

Gowans, Alan, *Architecture in New Jersey*, Princeton, D. Van Nostrand, 1964

——, *Images of American Living: Four Centuries of Architecture and Furniture as Cultural Expression*, Philadelphia, J. B. Lippincott, 1964

Hageman, John Frelinghuysen, *History of Princeton and Its Institutions*, 2 vols., Philadelphia, J. B. Lippincott, 1879

Hamlin, Talbot, *Benjamin Henry Latrobe*, New York, Oxford University Press, 1955

——, *Greek Revival Architecture in America*, New York, Oxford University Press, 1944

Harris, Frederick Morgan, "Taverns of Old Princeton," *Nassau Literary Magazine*, Jan. and Feb. 1907, LXII, 246-256, 287-298

Hinsdale, Horace Graham, *An Historical Discourse commemorating the Centenary of the Organization of the First Presbyterian Church, Princeton, N.J.*, Princeton, 1888

Hitchcock, Henry-Russell, *The Architecture of H. H. Richardson and His Times*, New York, The Museum of Modern Art, 1936

——, and Philip Johnson, *The International Style: Architecture since 1922*, New York, Norton, 1932

——, *American Architectural Books; a List of Books, Portfolios, and Pamphlets Published in America Before 1895*, Middletown, Conn., 1938-1939

Hodge, Archibald Alexander, *The Life of Charles Hodge*, New York, Charles Scribner's Sons, 1880

Howells, John Mead, *Lost Examples of Colonial Architecture*, New York, William Helburn, Inc., 1931

Kalm, Peter, *Travels in North America*, edited by Adolph B. Benson, New York, Wilson-Erickson, 1937

Kimball, Fiske, *American Architecture*, New York, Bobbs-Merrill, 1928

——, *Domestic Architecture of the American Colonies and of the Early Republic*, New York, Charles Scribner's Sons, 1922

Lafever, Minard, *The Beauties of Modern Architecture*, 3d ed., New York, D. Appleton & Co., 1839

Lane, Wheaton J., *From Indian Trail to Iron Horse*, Princeton, Princeton University Press, 1939

Langley, Batty, *City and Country Builder's and Workman's Treasury of Designs*, London, J. Ilive, 1740

Lundin, Leonard, *Cockpit of the Revolution: The War for Independence in New Jersey*, Princeton, Princeton University Press, 1940

Maas, John, *The Gingerbread Age*, New York, Rinehart & Co., 1957

Maclean, John, *History of the College of New Jersey*, 2 vols., Philadelphia, J. B. Lippincott & Co., 1877

McCormick, Richard P., *New Jersey from Colony to State*, Princeton, D. Van Nostrand, 1964

Miller, Samuel, *The Life of Samuel Miller*, Philadelphia, Claxton, Remsen & Haffelfinger, 1869

Monette, Orra Eugene, *First Settlers of Ye Plantations of Piscataway and Woodbridge, Olde East New Jersey, 1664-1714*, 7 vols., Los Angeles, 1930-1935

Moreau de Saint-Méry, *Voyage aux États-Unis de l'Amérique, 1793-1798*, ed. with intro. and notes by Stewart L. Mims, New Haven, Yale University Press, 1913

Morrison, Hugh, *Early American Architecture*, New York, Oxford University Press, 1952

Mumford, Lewis, *The Brown Decades*, 2d rev. ed., New York, Dover, 1955

——, *Sticks and Stones*, 2d rev. ed., New York, Dover, 1955

Nassau Hall, 1756-1956, edited by Henry Lyttleton Savage, Princeton, Princeton University, 1956

Norton, Paul F., "Latrobe and Old West at Dickinson College," *Art Bulletin*, June 1951, XXXIII, 125-132

Peterson, Charles, "Carpenters' Hall," *Historic Philadelphia*, Transactions of the American Philosophical Society, XLIII, 1, 1953, 96-128

Rice, Howard C., Jr., ed., *New Jersey Road Maps*, Princeton, Princeton University Library, 1964

Rush, Benjamin, *Letters*, edited by Lyman H. Butterfield, 2 vols., Princeton, Princeton University Press, 1951

Schuyler, Montgomery, *American Studies*, 2 vols., edited by William Jordy and Ralph Coe, Cambridge, Harvard University Press, 1961

——, "The Architecture of American Colleges: III, Princeton," *Architectural Record*, Feb. 1910, XXVII, 129-160

——, "The Work of William Appleton Potter," *Architectural Record*, Sept. 1909, XXVI, 176-196

Scully, Vincent J., *The Shingle Style*, New Haven, Yale University Press, 1955

Smith, Samuel, *The History of New Jersey*, 2d ed., Trenton, 1877

Stryker, William Scudder, *The Battles of Trenton and Princeton*, Boston, Houghton Mifflin, 1898

Tatum, George B., *Penn's Great Town*, Philadelphia, University of Pennsylvania Press, 1961

Tunnard, Christopher and Henry Hope Reed, *American Skyline*, Boston, Houghton Mifflin Co., 1956

Upjohn, Everard Miller, *Richard Upjohn, Architect and Churchman*, New York, Columbia University Press, 1939

Wallace, Paul A. W., "Historic Hope Lodge," *Pennsylvania Magazine of History and Biography*, April 1962, LXXXVI, 115-142

Waterman, Thomas Tileston, *The Dwellings of Colonial America*, Chapel Hill, University of North Carolina Press, 1950

Weiss, Harry B. and Grace Ziegler, *Colonel Erkuries Beatty, 1759-1823*, Trenton, The Past Times Press, 1958

Wertenbaker, Thomas Jefferson, *Princeton, 1746-1896*, Princeton, Princeton University Press, 1946

——, *The Founding of American Civilization: The Middle Colonies*, New York, Charles Scribner's Sons, 1949

Whitehill, Walter Muir, *The Arts in American History*, Chapel Hill, University of North Carolina Press, 1965

Wickes, Stephen, *History of Medicine in New Jersey*, Newark, Martin R. Dennis & Co., 1879

Williams, John Rogers, *The Handbook of Princeton*, New York, The Grafton Press, 1905

INDEX

Index